# WENTWORTH
# WOODHOUSE

*Dedicated to Melvyn Jones, who passed away in January 2021 and who sadly was unable to see this book in print.*

# WENTWORTH WOODHOUSE

## THE HOUSE, THE ESTATE AND THE FAMILY

**MELVYN JONES, JOAN JONES AND
STEPHEN COOPER**

PEN & SWORD
HISTORY

AN IMPRINT OF PEN & SWORD BOOKS LTD.
YORKSHIRE – PHILADELPHIA

First published in Great Britain in 2021 by
**PEN AND SWORD HISTORY**
An imprint of
Pen & Sword Books Ltd
Yorkshire - Philadelphia

ISBN 978 1 52678 301 1

Typeset in Times New Roman 10/12 by
SJmagic DESIGN SERVICES, India.
Printed and bound by CPI UK.

Pen & Sword Books Ltd incorporates the Imprints of Pen & Sword Archaeology,
Atlas, Aviation, Battleground, Discovery, Family History, History, Maritime, Military,
Naval, Politics, Railways, Select, Transport, True Crime, Fiction, Frontline Books, Leo
Cooper, Praetorian Press, Seaforth Publishing, Wharncliffe and White Owl.

For a complete list of Pen & Sword titles please contact

PEN & SWORD BOOKS LIMITED
47 Church Street, Barnsley, South Yorkshire, S70 2AS, England
E-mail: enquiries@pen-and-sword.co.uk
Website: www.pen-and-sword.co.uk

or

PEN AND SWORD BOOKS
1950 Lawrence Rd, Havertown, PA 19083, USA
E-mail: uspen-and-sword@casematepublishers.com
Website: www.penandswordbooks.com

# Contents

# ACKNOWLEDGEMENTS

W e are grateful for the help we have been given over the years by the staff of Sheffield Archives and Rotherham Local Studies and Archives. We acknowledge the permission of Olive, Countess Fitzwilliam's Wentworth Settlement Trustees and Sheffield City Archives for access to, permission to quote from and to reproduce two images from the Wentworth Woodhouse Muniments in Sheffield Archives. We would also like to thank James Saunders Watson of Rockingham Castle for his permission to use the portrait of Thomas Watson-Wentworth that hangs in the castle, and Sir Anthony Cooke-Yarborough for allowing us to use material from the journal kept by George Eustace Cooke-Yarborough, which is held in Doncaster Archives. Our thanks also go to Val Bintcliffe, Chapeltown & High Green Archive, Kevin Lee, Val Sykes and Wentworth Woodhouse Preservation Trust. Unless otherwise stated, the images are from the authors' collections.

**The Palladian front of Wentworth Woodhouse.**

# INTRODUCTION

Selecting the contents of this book has been very difficult. There is such a wealth of material on the house, the estate and the family from all periods. And this research material comes in so many forms: the estate and family papers in record offices (principally Sheffield Archives), census data, newspaper accounts, oral recollections, photographs and maps, and the work of other researchers on the estate and the family.

A second issue has been how to organise the contents. In the end we have chosen a chronological/thematic approach. Chronologically, the contents start in the last decade of the sixteenth century with the birth of Thomas Wentworth, the future 1st Earl of Strafford, and end with the acquisition of the mansion by the Wentworth Woodhouse Preservation Trust in 2017. In terms of themes, the careers, concerns and preoccupations of heads of the family – the 1st Earl of Strafford, Thomas Watson-Wentworth, the 1st and 2nd Marquises of Rockingham and the 7th Earl Fitzwilliam – are the subject of Chapters 1, 2, 3, 4, 5 and 9 respectively; the house is central to Chapters 11 and 12; the estate is discussed in detail in chapters 6 and 7; and family celebrations in Chapter 10. The attitudes of the family to their employees and tenants are dealt with in Chapter 8. We hope this book will encourage you to investigate further the historical records, explore the house and treasure the surrounding historic landscape. Read on and enjoy.

F. P. 505. Terrilorial Sports, Wentworth, May 13. 1913. Viscount Milton In Wheelbarrow Race.

**Peter (the future 8th Earl) about to enter the wheelbarrow race.**

# WENTWORTH WOODHOUSE HISTORICAL TIMELINE 1593–2017

| | |
|---|---|
| **1593** | Thomas Wentworth (later 1st Earl of Strafford) born. |
| **1614** | Thomas Wentworth succeeds his father as head of the Wentworth estate. |
| **1633** | Thomas Wentworth appointed to be Lord Deputy of Ireland. Acquires large properties in County Wicklow. |
| **1640** | Thomas Wentworth created Earl of Strafford. |
| **1641** | Earl of Strafford executed. |
| **1695** | On the death of William, 2nd Earl of Strafford, the Wentworth estate is inherited by Thomas Watson, third son of the 2nd Earl's sister. The will required that he change his name to Thomas Watson-Wentworth. |
| **1723** | On the death of Thomas Watson-Wentworth, he is succeeded by his only surviving son, Thomas Wentworth, who is created the 1st Marquis of Rockingham in 1747. |
| **1724** | The future 1st Marquis begins building the Baroque mansion. |
| **1732** | The future 1st Marquis begins building the Palladian mansion. |
| **1748** | The 1st Marquis completes Hoober Stand. |
| **1750** | By the time of the death of the 1st Marquis he has spent £90,000 on his building projects, and on extending and landscaping the park. He is succeeded by his son, Charles, who becomes the 2nd Marquis of Rockingham. |
| **1751** | The 2nd Marquis marries Mary Bright. |
| **1765–66** | The 2nd Marquis of Rockingham becomes Prime Minister. |
| **1768–89** | The Stable Block, designed by John Carr, is built. |
| **1773–80** | Keppel's Column erected. |
| **1782** | The 2nd Marquis of Rockingham becomes Prime Minister again but dies in office. As he is childless his estates are inherited by his nephew, the 4th Earl Fitzwilliam. |
| **1788** | The Mausoleum is completed in Wentworth Park in memory of the 2nd Marquis of Rockingham. |
| **1790s** | By this time, industrial development on the estate is in full swing: coal mining at Elsecar Colliery, ironstone mining at Tankersley and the Elsecar and Milton Ironworks opened. Expansion of Elsecar village is under way. |
| **1833** | The 4th Earl dies and he is succeeded by his son, Charles William, 5th Earl Fitzwilliam. |
| **1847** | The beginning of a nine-year scheme to aid financially emigrants to Canada from the Irish estate during the Great Famine. 6,000 tenants and their families migrate. |

| | |
|---|---|
| **1857** | The 5th Earl Fitzwilliam dies and he is succeeded by his son, William, the 6th Earl Fitzwilliam. |
| **1888** | The 6th Earl and Countess Fitzwilliam celebrate their Golden Wedding. |
| **1902** | The 6th Earl dies and is succeeded by his grandson, William, who becomes the 7th Earl Fitzwilliam. |
| **1911** | Elaborate christening celebrations for Peter (the future 8th Earl). The 7th Earl and Countess had already had four daughters. |
| **1943** | The 7th Earl dies and is succeeded by Peter, the 8th Earl Fitzwilliam. |
| **1946** | Opencast coal mining begins in the grounds of Wentworth Woodhouse. |
| **1948** | Peter, the 8th Earl is killed in an aircraft accident. In the absence of a son, the earldom passes to Eric, a cousin, who becomes the 9th Earl. |
| **1950** | The 9th Earl occupies rooms at Wentworth Woodhouse but this is not his principal residence. Most of the mansion and the stable block are occupied by the Lady Mabel College of Education. |
| **1952** | Eric dies without issue and the earldom passes to Thomas, son of George Fitzwilliam of Milton. |
| **1979** | Thomas, the 10th Earl, dies without issue and the earldom becomes extinct. After amalgamation of Lady Mabel College with Sheffield City Polytechnic in 1976, the mansion and stable block continue to be occupied by the Polytechnic until 1986. |
| **1989** | The mansion is sold to Wensley Haydon-Baillie. |
| **1999** | The mansion is bought by the Newbold family, who occupy it until 2017. They carry out restoration work and start tours of the mansion for the public. |
| **2017** | The Newbolds sell the mansion to the Wentworth Woodhouse Preservation Trust following a grant of £7.9 million by the Chancellor of the Exchequer. |

*Chapter 1*

# THE 1ST EARL OF STRAFFORD

**The man and his family**

The Earldom of Strafford derives its name from the Strafforth Wapentake, which was a district of the County of Yorkshire, and is more specifically associated with what we now call South Yorkshire. We are concerned here with the person for whom the title was first created, in 1640, Sir Thomas Wentworth of Wentworth Woodhouse (1593–1641). There were two Earls of Strafford of the first creation in the seventeenth century and three Earls of Strafford of the second creation in the eighteenth century, and to date, there have been nine such earls of the third creation. The descendants of the earls of the first creation had their seat at Wentworth Woodhouse, near Rotherham, until 1950, while the descendants of the earls of the second creation had theirs at Wentworth Castle, near Barnsley, until 1948. The public house known as the Earl of Strafford at Hooton Roberts was once the dower house of the family at Wentworth Woodhouse, and the public house known as the Strafford Arms at Stainborough was named after the family at Wentworth Castle.

Returning to the 1st Earl of the first creation, he was far and away the most famous of them all. He was the eldest son of Sir William Wentworth and Anna (née Atkinson) and had seven brothers and three sisters, as depicted in the memorial in Wentworth old church. He is usually referred to as Strafford rather than Sir Thomas Wentworth, although he was only made a peer in the last year of his life. Thomas Wentworth (as he then was) was knighted in 1611 at the age of 18. He went on a tour of France for fourteen months and learned French. He succeeded his father as baronet and owner of Wentworth Woodhouse in 1614, at the age of 21. He also became the guardian of nine younger brothers and sisters. He was a careful steward of the estates in Yorkshire but on occasion ran into debt through speculative buying of land and entrepreneurial ventures. He always felt at home at Wentworth and in a letter written from there in 1623, wrote:

> our objects and thoughts are limited to looking upon a tulip, hearing a bird sing, a rivulet murmuring, or some such petty, yet innocent pastime. By my troth, I wish you, divested of the importunity of business, here for half a dozen hours: you should taste how free and fresh we breathe …[1]

He married three times. In 1611 he married Lady Margaret Clifford, daughter of the Earl of Cumberland, but she died childless in 1622. In 1625 he married Lady Arabella Holles, daughter of the Earl of Clare. They had a son, William, who became the 2nd Earl

**Thomas, 1st Earl of Strafford, with Sir Philip Mainwaring, Secretary of State. Engraving made from a painting by Anthony van Dyck.** *Freemantle, 1911*

of Strafford, and two daughters, Ann and Arabella, and a son, Thomas, who died in infancy. Strafford's second wife died in 1631. His third wife was Elizabeth, daughter of Sir Godfrey Rhodes of Great Houghton. They married in 1632 and had one daughter, Margaret. After his death, his third wife went to live in the estate dower house at Hooton Roberts. She died in 1688.

Strafford became an MP, was a prominent critic of King Charles I and a supporter of the Petition of Right of 1628, which sought to limit the King's prerogative powers. In 1629, after Parliament had been prorogued and then dissolved, he changed sides, and served Charles during what the Puritans later damned as 'the Eleven Years' Tyranny'. He was Lord President of the Council of the North and Lord Deputy of Ireland. He managed to alienate all existing interest groups in Ireland. Was he corrupt? No more than the next man, given the fact that civil servants were not paid. But historian Dame Veronica Wedgwood's biography of him, in its 2nd edition (1961), makes it clear that he set out to acquire the Irish estates by fair means and foul.[2]

His Irish estates were in seven distinct blocks. One of these, in the half barony of Sligo, was sold by the 2nd Earl's executors in 1695 to help pay the 2nd Earl's debts and legacies. The other six – Naas in County Kildare, and Newcastle, Wicklow Town, Rathdrum, Cashaw and Shillelagh in County Wicklow – amounting to 90,000 acres (36,423 hectares), remained in the possession of the Wentworth estate until the Wyndham Land Act of 1903. The Naas estate in County Kildare comprised 1,458 acres (590 hectares). It was on the high road to Dublin, near an ancient market town. Today the ruins of the 1st Earl of Strafford's Jigginstown House, built during the 1630s, still survive. It was built of brick and was 380 feet (116 metres) long. The two properties near the Wicklow coast, Newcastle and Wicklow Town, had originally been plantation land granted to the Earl of Carlisle and came into the possession of the 1st Earl of Strafford by royal grant between 1638 and 1640. The Rathdrum property was purchased in 1637 from William Graham and his partners. It lay on the flanks of the Wicklow Mountains. The fifth and largest of Strafford's property was made up of the adjacent properties of Cashaw and Shillelagh, with an outlier at Toorboy. It covered just over 74,000 acres – 18 per cent of the county and 83 per cent of the Irish estate. Cashaw was purchased from William Graham in 1637 and Shillelagh from Calcott Chambers' estate in 1638.

### Wentworth Woodhouse in Strafford's day

Strafford's main seat in England, at Wentworth Woodhouse, was almost completely rebuilt in the eighteenth century, but a surviving etching purporting to be of his mansion appeared in Joseph Hunter's *South Yorkshire* in 1831, and is said to be based

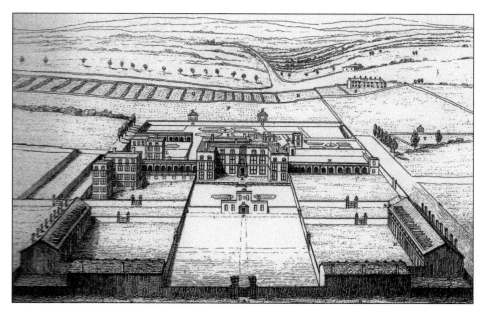

**Etching of 'Old Wentworth House' in the seventeenth century, made from an oil painting.**
*Hunter, 1831*

on a painting in Wentworth Woodhouse.[3] Besides the main residence, the etching shows stables, a porter's lodge, the kitchen, towers, an orangery, two summer houses, the kitchen garden and knot gardens.

Almost nothing remains of the 1st Earl's house, apart from the brickwork at the south end of the present house, surrounding the Old Hall on the ground floor and the Yellow Bedroom on the first floor. The Old Hall now presents itself as the Billiard Room as it was around 1900, but there is some evidence that billiards was played in Strafford's time, since part of his billiard table was used to frame a Bible and a prayer book carried to the scaffold by Charles I in 1649.[4] As for the Yellow Bedroom, it is sometimes said that it was from here that Strafford learnt that he was to be executed. This is not quite true, but he was certainly at home when he was summoned to London in November 1640 to face the impeachment proceedings, and he wrote to a friend:

> I am tomorrow to London, with more danger beset, I believe, than ever man went out of Yorkshire; yet my heart is good and I can find nothing cold within me.

He also said, 'I am pulled from old Woodhouse by head and ears.' Legend has it that he was arrested hiding in an oak tree in nearby Tankersley Park. This tree was identified on the first edition of the Ordnance Survey 6-inch map of the 1850s.

At one time, the house had many fine paintings, including van Dycks. This demonstrated Strafford's importance, since only a man at the very highest levels of government could have had his portrait painted by Sir Anthony van Dyck, who was Charles I's court painter. In addition, Strafford was a great collector, and had many other fine artefacts. These were kept at Wentworth Woodhouse until 1979, when the collection was removed by Lady Juliet, the only daughter of Peter, the 8th Earl, who had been killed in the infamous flying accident with Kathleen ('Kick') Kennedy in 1948. The Earl had no male heir and, as a woman, Lady Juliet could inherit the paintings, but not the earldom or the entailed estates.

Wentworth Woodhouse lay at the centre of a substantial home estate in South Yorkshire. A list of the household at Wentworth Woodhouse compiled shortly after Strafford inherited the estate identifies sixty-four individuals including family, visitors and servants. Mr (Richard) Marris (see below) is listed. He was the steward in charge at that time. Dame Veronica Wedgwood's first biography of Strafford, published in 1935,[5] held Strafford in high regard. However, as she tells us in the introduction to the second edition of her book, published in 1961, she had become aware of a mass of new evidence, including the vast resource that is the Wentworth Woodhouse Muniments deposited in Sheffield Archives. As a result, Wedgwood looked more closely at Strafford's failings.

Richard Marris makes several appearances in Wedgwood's book, opportunities she uses to shed light on both the good and bad sides of his master's character. She revealed that a friendship had developed between the two men. It appears that rather than going to dinner with his aristocratic neighbours, Strafford preferred to sit down with Marris, enjoy a pipe and discuss agricultural projects with him. However, Wedgwood also noted

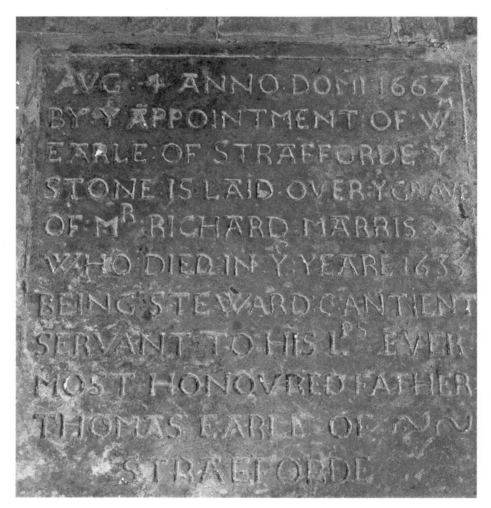

**Richard Marris's gravestone in Wentworth old church.**

that the steward was 'an inveterate and excessive drinker'. She thought that this was a vice that Strafford disapproved of, since he was always something of a Puritan.

In June 1636, Strafford heard that Marris had drowned while crossing a stream in Yorkshire in a drunken condition. This cannot have come as a complete surprise because he had already warned the man about his drinking, but when he returned to Wentworth, he found that his estates had been much neglected. He took up residence in Covent Garden for a time, attended on the King, had his portrait painted by van Dyck and made a statement in Westminster, arguing that there had been a 'marvellous improvement' in the state of Ireland since he had become Deputy. He was now seen by many as potentially 'the greatest man in England'. Meanwhile, he arranged for his erstwhile steward to be buried in Wentworth old church, and commemorated by a tombstone, which still survives. The inscription records that Marris was Strafford's 'Steward and Antient Servant'.

## Strafford's demise

Strafford's role in the build-up to the English Civil War of 1642–46 was crucial. During the 1630s, he was Charles I's mainstay in the North of England and in Ireland, and it looked as if his policies were working. In 1640, Charles even asked him to take charge of central government, but their scheme for ruling without Parliament broke down as a result of the Bishops' Wars in Scotland. Charles had to recall Parliament, and the House of Commons was united in calling for the impeachment of Strafford. The Commons regarded their former colleague and champion as a turncoat (hence his nickname 'Black Tom Tyrant'). The main allegation was that he had conspired to put the English Parliament down by force. He had indeed written to the King, telling him, 'You have an army in Ireland you may employ to reduce *this kingdom* [author's italics],' but it is overwhelmingly likely that Strafford was referring to the Kingdom of Scotland at this time.

When the impeachment proceedings faltered, the Commons duly brought forward a bill of attainder. Strafford defended himself once more in the House of Lords. He asked how a number of mere misdemeanours could amount to high treason and pointed out that there was no precedent for executing a man for mere words – and all he had allegedly done was threaten to bring over an Irish army, and there was no treasonous intent. He argued that Parliament should hesitate to invent new capital offences in this way.[6] The Earl of Bedford was against the attainder and sought to moderate the violent opinions of some of his fellow peers, but the Earl of Essex's answer was chilling: 'Stone Dead hath no Fellow.'[7] On 19 April, the Commons declared Strafford a traitor and two days later, the House passed the bill of attainder by a majority of 204 to 59. The King wrote to Strafford, promising him his life:

> I must lay by the thought of employing you hereafter in my affairs, yet I assure you now, in the midst of your troubles, that, upon the word of a King, you shall not suffer in life, honour, or fortune.

**Black Tom inn sign in Tinahely, County Wicklow, Ireland.**

**One of a series of contemporary woodcuts depicting the beheading of the 1st Earl of Strafford in 1641.** *Freemantle, 1911*

The next day, a mob beset the House of Lords, crying for justice, and posted up the names of the fifty-nine MPs who had voted against the bill of attainder as traitors to their country. The bill became an Act, which provided that Strafford be hung, drawn and quartered, like a common traitor, but at the last, he was granted the 'privilege' of death by beheading. Strafford told the King that he should no longer feel bound to spare his life, but asked that he be allowed to die in private. This was beyond Charles's power, and Strafford's head was struck off in public.

### Where was the 1st Earl of Strafford buried?

There is a monument, believed by Pevsner and Harman to have been erected *c.* 1689, to the Earl in Wentworth old church,[8] but the inscription does not state that he is buried there. Thorough examinations of the interior and exterior of Wentworth old church over the years have failed to find Strafford's tomb, and the family vault was not constructed until 1825. Legends grew up that he had been buried elsewhere to prevent his grave from being desecrated. Some even said that he was interred 8 miles away, at Hooton Roberts (where his widow, who survived him by forty-seven years, lived until she died). Lady Margaret Wentworth, their daughter, also died there in 1681. In Dame Veronica Wedgwood's view, this story is baseless. And furthermore, in a letter of uncertain origin dated 1923, a member of the family, Albreda, said that her sister Mary told her not long before she died that her parents (the 6th Earl and Countess

Fitzwilliam) had Lord Strafford's grave in Wentworth old church opened and found the body, with the head severed.[9]

However, twenty years earlier, in an article in the *Cornhill Magazine* in July 1905, the Reverend Reginald Gatty wrote that during repairs being carried out in the chancel of St John the Baptist church at Hooton Roberts in 1895, a 2-foot deep trench had been dug and revealed the remains of two badly decomposed bodies, and a casket carrying a skeleton.[10] After Gatty was called to look at the remains, one of the workmen pointed out that one of the vertebrae had been cut clean in half. When the two other bodies were examined by a surgeon, Gatty claimed that they belonged to an old woman and a girl of about 16. These were believed to be Lady Strafford and her daughter. However, the daughter had been in her early forties when she died. Gatty took photographs of the skulls but not the sliced vertebra.

Again, what must be emphasised is that no tomb for Strafford is known to exist in the precincts of Wentworth old church, the monument in the old church was not erected until nearly fifty years after the execution, and that Reginald Gatty was not only a clergyman but a respected archaeologist. Whether one of the bodies exhumed at Hooton Roberts was Strafford must be presumed unknown until the bodies are exhumed again and a forensic examination has taken place. The mystery of the place of Strafford's interment continues to divide researchers. In a more recent review of the evidence, local historian Christopher Morley was of the opinion that failing a forensic examination of the Hooton Roberts' remains, we may have to wait for someone to be on hand in the churchyard to witness the raising of the dead upon the sound of the last trumpet![11]

### What happened after Strafford's execution?

With Strafford out of the way, Charles I drifted, but so did the House of Commons. One could even say that their attempt to 'take back control' was a failure, and having eliminated the threat from Strafford, they were hopelessly divided as to what to do next. The impasse led to war because a majority wanted to take control of the army, and Charles I was prepared to fight, rather than agree. He raised his standard at Nottingham and men began to rally to one side or the other, each raising forces of their own.

The First English Civil War of 1642–46 (which almost everyone has heard of) was followed by a Second Civil War in 1648. Although almost no one has heard of it, it was this war that led to the formation of the one and only English Republic. Contrary to what is popularly believed, nobody had wanted to execute the King when the First Civil War broke out. However, by 1649, there was an important section of opinion that demanded that the King be brought to justice, and Oliver Cromwell in particular thought that the King's conduct in reaching an understanding with the Scots was unforgiveable because it had been an attempt to 'vassalize us to a foreign nation'.

The charge against the King stated that he:

> hath traitorously and maliciously levied war against the present Parliament, and the people therein represented. The indictment stated that he was guilty of all the treasons, murders, rapines, burnings, spoils, desolations, damages and mischiefs to this nation, acted and committed in the said wars, or occasioned thereby.

This was a new and peculiar kind of treason, since the Treason Act of 1351 (still used in the twentieth century) required that the accused had to be involved in some act prejudicial to the King or his immediate family, rather than the nation at large. Nonetheless, a special court, consisting of several dozen commissioners and presided over by John Bradshaw, was set up. The trial began on 20 January 1649 in Westminster Hall. Charles refused to enter a plea, claiming that no court had jurisdiction over a monarch. He argued that as anointed king, he ruled by virtue of the Divine Right of Kings and by the traditions and laws of England, and that the court was illegitimate. Moreover, the trial was illegal, since the King was the fount of all justice and could do no wrong. The House of Commons – purged of dissent, and without the House of Lords – could not try anybody, and certainly not him. The result was that the court decided to proceed as if he had pleaded guilty, though thirty witnesses were still summoned for 'the further and clearer satisfaction of their own judgment and consciences'. Charles did not stay to hear their evidence.

The King was declared guilty on Saturday, 27 January 1649, and was sentenced to death. To show unanimity, all sixty-seven commissioners rose to their feet. The death warrant was eventually signed by fifty-nine, including two who had not been present when the sentence was passed. The King was beheaded in front of the Banqueting House in Whitehall. Strafford's execution, and his own part in it, must have been much on his mind. His last words included the thought that God had permitted his own execution as a punishment for consenting to the Earl's death.

### John Marris

Richard Marris had a grandson, John. He was born in Elmsall but brought up in Wentworth, probably as a page. When Strafford became Lord Deputy of Ireland in 1632, John was only 16, but was nevertheless made ensign in his master's company of foot, and soon afterwards lieutenant of his guard. During the Irish Rebellion of 1641, he helped to defend the town of Drogheda against attack by Irish rebels. Meanwhile, civil war had broken out in England. During the English Civil War of 1642–46, Marris was a Royalist, although he briefly turned his coat when Liverpool surrendered to a parliamentary army, but always denied that he was responsible for betraying the port. He then retired to Elmsall and started to plan how he could help the Royalists once more.[12]

In May 1648, the Royalists captured Pontefract Castle. One of the Cavalier leaders on this occasion was none other than John Marris. Marris and his men had achieved a remarkable success. He appointed officers to command foot and horse soldiers both inside the castle walls and in the town of Pontefract, where Marris quartered some troops. His coup was so successful that he seems to have captured most of the parliamentary garrison. The taking of Pontefract Castle gave heart to Royalists everywhere and, from the parliamentary point of view, it was important to retake it.

Oliver Cromwell arrived back at Pontefract on Friday, 3 November 1648. On 9 November, he sent a summons to Marris asking him to surrender, or else the castle would be taken by storm. Marris refused to recognise Cromwell's authority, and did not even tell his own men about the summons. In the middle of January, it was known that King Charles was to be tried at Westminster, but the Cavaliers in Pontefract refused to give up, even when they heard the shattering news that the King – in whose name they held the castle – had indeed been executed. Instead, they minted silver coins with Charles II's name and likeness on them.[13] However, they must also have known in their hearts that their days were numbered – and we soon learn that negotiations had begun.

At the beginning of February, John Marris asked for terms. Soon afterwards, he received a reply, which proposed that a general indemnity be granted to the Royalists, with six named exceptions – of whom Marris was one. Marris and the five other condemned men escaped but were captured in Lancashire about ten days later.

There was a delay of some months between Marris's capture in Lancashire and his trial in York. This began on 16 August 1649, when he was indicted under the Treason Act of 1351 'for levying war against the late King Charles'. He and a fellow prisoner, Blackborne, managed to escape from York Castle, but Blackborne broke a leg in doing so and Marris refused to abandon him. Like Strafford in 1641, and like King Charles earlier in 1649, Marris was beheaded. His body – or what was left of it – was buried at Wentworth, 'near unto the grave of his worthy lord and master the late famous Earle of Strafford'.[14] He was 34 years of age.

*Chapter 2*

# … ACROSS THE SEA TO IRELAND

**Thomas Watson-Wentworth's visit to his Irish estates in 1713**
An investigation in Sheffield Archives into the ways in which the coppice woods on the Irish estate of Thomas Watson-Wentworth (1665–1723) were managed revealed detailed entries in the estate account books of a trip he made in the early 1700s to his distant Irish estates. It must be emphasised to any reader who has not perused account books that they are not just boring lists of figures; they contain some fascinating information that can be used with other archive documents to paint a vivid picture of a place, a time and people. Because account books deal with money, either being received or paid out, no detail is spared. The records analysed here show the hands-on approach of Thomas Watson-Wentworth in the management of his estates and also throw light on topics such as early travel, taking precautions against the activities of highwaymen, the transformation of the landscape, and attitudes towards tenants and estate workers.[1]

**The landowner and his estates**
Thomas Watson inherited the estates of the 2nd Earl of Strafford, who had died childless in 1695. It was a surprising inheritance because Thomas was not his son but his nephew, the third son of the Earl's sister, Anne Wentworth, who had married Edward Watson, 2nd Baron Rockingham of Rockingham Castle in Northamptonshire. The will stipulated that on his inheritance he had to live permanently at Wentworth Woodhouse and change his name from Thomas Watson to Thomas Watson-Wentworth. His descendants were the 1st and 2nd Marquises of Rockingham and the Earls Fitzwilliam.

The estates that he inherited were immense. In South Yorkshire, surrounding Wentworth House was a compact estate covering 9,000 acres (3,642 hectares). Not only did this estate contain farmland, it also had more than two dozen productive coppice woods, and beneath the ground there were extensive seams of ironstone and coal that would be exploited for great profit by Thomas Watson-Wentworth's descendants for more than two centuries. Thomas Watson-Wentworth devoted much time extending his South Yorkshire estate, making forty-two separate purchases and adding another 1,641 acres (664 hectares).[2] He also inherited a vast acreage in Ireland that had been acquired by his great-uncle, the 1st Earl of Strafford, from 1633 to 1640. The properties had the geographical advantage of lying near the County Wicklow coast and being 12–37 miles (19–60 kilometres) from Dublin. There was a small estate in County Kildare but the rest was in County Wicklow, in five blocks at Newcastle, Wicklow Town, Rathdrum, Toorboy, Cashaw and Shillelagh

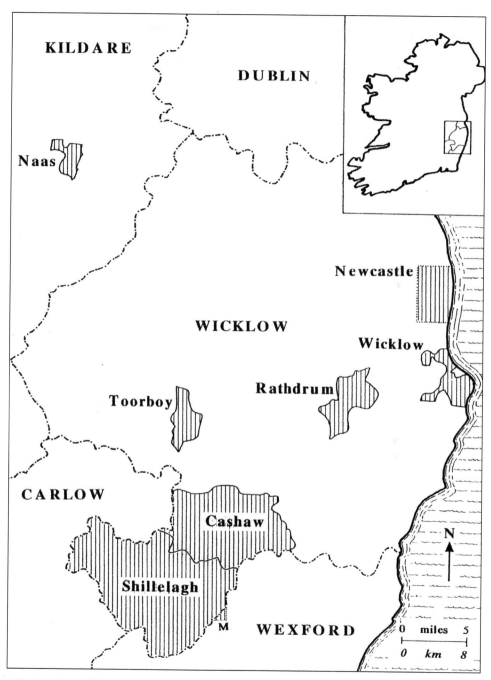

**The location of Thomas Watson-Wentworth's Irish estates.**

(see Chapter 1). Altogether, the Irish estates amounted to 90,000 acres (36,423 hectares). These Irish properties would remain in the ownership of the Wentworth-Fitzwilliams until 1903, when, under the terms of the Wyndham Land Act, all the tenanted properties were purchased by tenants with financial help from the government. All that remained was Coollattin House and the demesne land (the surrounding parkland and Home Farm). To put the importance of the Irish estates in the eighteenth century into their overall context, in 1723, the year in which Thomas Watson-Wentworth died, the annual income from all his properties amounted to about £16,000. Of that, more than £6,000 accrued from his Irish estates, i.e. 38 per cent of his total income.

The purpose of Thomas's journey to Ireland in 1713 was to inspect his estates, particularly his woodlands (which provided not only building materials but also charcoal for iron smelting and oak bark for tanneries, and therefore a considerable income) and to set new tenancies on the farmed estate properties. These were made chiefly to Protestant settlers (sometimes called chief tenants or middlemen) who then in most cases sublet parts of their rented property to undertenants. The smallest tenancies were those occupied by Irish Roman Catholic smallholders. Thomas was very particular about the tenancies to chief tenants, insisting that improvements were made such as to buildings, enclosing farmland and planting trees. He was also keen to establish estate villages, where craftsmen and shopkeepers lived and a substantial number of new schools and churches were built during his landlordship.

### The journey to Ireland
Thomas Watson-Wentworth probably left Wentworth House towards the end of the second week in August 1713. He was not alone; he was accompanied by a number of servants who were to go with him to Ireland, together with others who were making the journey to the port of embarkation and then returning to Wentworth. They were probably in charge of a coach that contained enough luggage for a protracted stay. As we shall see, he took his own riding horses with him, so besides personal servants he would also have had the services of a groom. Only one of his servants can be identified: Matthew Charlton, who is buried at Hooton Roberts just 5 miles from Wentworth, where his gravestone is fixed to the outside of the church wall. The direction of Thomas's journey over the Pennines must remain a mystery; no records have survived. However, it is possible to suggest a route. From Wentworth the party would probably have picked up the ancient saltway between Rotherham and Cheshire via the Flouch, over Saltersbrook and then via Woodhead and Tintwistle as far as Altrincham, and then travelled along the old Roman Road between Manchester and Chester. The journey would have taken about three days, with two overnight stops. Parts of the way were packhorse routes and his coach may have had to be pulled out of deep mud if there had been any heavy rain.

A letter he had posted to his principal Irish agent before he left England had been sent from Chester, so it is almost certainly this port from which he embarked on his sea crossing to Ireland. The ship would, of course, have been a sailing ship dependent on the wind, so that the date of sailing, the duration of the journey and the date of arrival would only have been known approximately. This is borne out by

**Crossing the Pennines.** *Eric Leslie*

the entries in his principal agent's (Captain Abraham Nickson) accounts itemising his expenses as he waited for his employer – referred to as 'my master' or 'his Honour' – to arrive. Altogether, Nickson went to Ringsend, the port area of Dublin, five times from 16 to 25 August. On the fourth of these visits, on 23 August, he went to Lazy Hill, from which there was a good view of the harbour and incoming vessels. He then went down to Ringsend, where he waited in vain for two hours. He went again on 25 August, but there was still no sign, so he returned to his lodgings in Dublin. Then a messenger came to say the ship had arrived. He went to greet his employer, recording in his accounts that he had paid 'the sea men yt slung his Honrs Horses to shore' and for the hire of a car (a two-wheeled cart) to carry his employer's 'Portmantle, Sadles etc'. He also paid for two coaches that went to Ringsend 'to receive his Honr from England' and for a load of straw and two barrels of white oats for the horses.

### Thomas Watson-Wentworth's stay in Ireland

Nickson had taken lodgings for Thomas Watson-Wentworth and his servants in Jervis Street in the centre of Dublin. The lodgings included a stable and a coach house. Having installed them there, he arranged for copies of the Irish estate papers to be brought from two secure rooms 'at Mr John Kennedy's in High Street, Dublin', where they were permanently stored. They were said to be in trunks and a chest of drawers. He recorded that he had paid a locksmith 'for mending the Locks on his Honrs Chest of Drawers'. He also bought 'one Quire of paper and penns for his Honr'. There are no records of what happened over the next few days but no doubt they were largely taken up with meetings between Thomas Watson-Wentworth and Nickson about estate matters.

Eventually they set off on horseback to the headquarters of the largest section of the estate at Coollattin in southern County Wicklow, a journey of more than 40 miles. Before they set off, the estate clerk, Joseph Waterhouse, together with Captain Nickson's cousin, Joshua (who assisted Captain Nickson in running the Shillelagh and Cashaw parts of the estate), and two trusted employees, Edward Smith and Abraham Slater, had arrived in Dublin carrying more than £600 destined for England. On such trips these men were heavily armed. In 1712, it was recorded in the accounts that a payment had been made for mending a 'double barreld Carbine in ordr to Guard ye moneys' because Nickson had reported that a man had been killed by robbers on the road between Dublin and Coollattin. And five years later, Nickson recorded in his Timber Accounts that he had 'Paid for Powder & Shott & Balls in ordr for our defence against raparees yt now Infest ye Roads'. 'Rapparee' was the Irish name for a bandit or highwayman. This armed party provided the escort for Thomas Watson-Wentworth when he set off to 'view his estate'. They must have formed a colourful and purposeful group. They were about twelve in number. They went south-west out of Dublin, skirting the northern fringes of the Wicklow Mountains. Nickson recorded that they stopped for 'a Bate at Ballymore'. 'Bait' is an archaic word meaning to stop on a journey to take food and rest. Ballymore Eustace is a good 25 miles from Dublin and was probably an overnight stop.

**The armed escort.** *Eric Leslie*

For the rest of September, Thomas Watson-Wentworth was based at Nickson's old house set in the park at Coollattin, near Shillelagh. In 1711, Nickson had recorded that he was building a new house and Watson-Wentworth gave Nickson £100 towards building costs. This new house was described in a survey of 1730 as 'built by ye late Capt. Nickson about 18 years ago and ye gardens laid out very beautifully … ye House and Outhouses well built and well furnished' with 'a Considerable quantity of ye land about ye House covered with young oaks and other trees'. From the base at Abraham Nickson's house at Coollattin, Thomas Watson-Wentworth would have had a busy time inspecting properties and his managed woods, and setting new leases. As well as inspecting his properties he would also have met tenants and other estate workers. On two occasions, Nickson recorded that Thomas Watson-Wentworth gave money to poor people who they encountered. On 6 September, for example, Nickson recorded that threepence was 'Given to the Poor on my Masters Orders', and on 11 September, 'fivepence was given to Edmund Byrne when His Honr was at Inverboy'.

In the eighteenth century, which was part of a period that became known as the 'Protestant Ascendancy', the native Irish Catholic population was regarded as disloyal to the Crown and was subject to a number of penal laws. They were forbidden to own land, to hold mortgages on land or hold long leases. And as with many other absentee Irish landlords, Thomas Watson-Wentworth, like his family before and after him, stuck rigidly to a politically circumscribed leasing policy and continued to lease to some

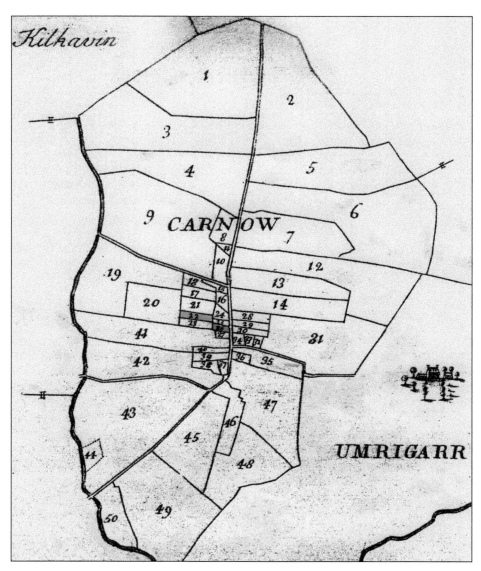

**The estate village of Carnew in 1728 showing individual tenanted plots of farmland and house plots. The Walker smallholding and house plot are shaded.** *Wentworth Woodhouse Muniments, WWM MP 96*

non-resident and residing Protestant chief tenants of substance who showed little inclination to improve beyond the boundaries of their demesnes.

It would be interesting to know what abiding impressions Thomas Watson-Wentworth took home with him after visiting very different parts of his estate. On 11 September, he was at the outlying property of Toorboy, high in the Wicklow Mountains at nearly 2,000 feet, inspecting the tenancies before setting new ones. His tenancies were usually for twenty-one years. There were three properties there that were described in two surveys done in 1728 and about 1730, less than twenty years after Thomas Watson-Wentworth's 1713 visit.[3] On one of these properties, which covered more than 1,490 acres, the chief tenant was Alexander Straghan. He was said to live in Dublin and let his property to eleven Catholic undertenants, who no doubt lived in small one-storey cabins with stone or sod walls and thatched roofs. The total population was seventy-four. The surveys give the first names and surnames of every male undertenant and the number of their children, and whether these were sons or daughters. The property was said to be 'mountainy', would not grow corn and the tenants were 'entirely maintained by potatoes'. One of the other two of these upland properties was tenanted by John Kinch, a Protestant, who 'dwelleth upon the land' and had six Roman Catholic undertenants. He was said to be an industrious man, improving the property little by little even though it contained much bog and boggy pasture.

In complete contrast to these two properties were two others visited by Thomas Watson-Wentworth and his principal agent in September 1713 that lay on the lower, better farmland in the valley of the river Derry. The first was Raheengraney, 6 miles south-west of Coollattin. This 344 acre property in 1730, seventeen years after Thomas-Watson Wentworth's visit, was tenanted by James Parsley, who was said to be 'the best improving tenant' on the estate. He sublet parts of the property to fifteen undertenants. In 1730, it was said to have been 'well improved' and was 'fit for ploughing and grazing with Extraordinary good meadows'. The second was Cronyhorn, a property of more than 600 acres, just to the west of the estate village of Carnew. According to the survey of 1730, the chief tenant was Walter Carter, who was resident in what was described as 'a very good house'. He was also a leather tanner with his tannery on the property. He had ten undertenants. With their dependants, the number of people living on the property in 1730 added up to fifty-three, the majority of whom had Irish, not English, names. The property was described as having 'the best & greatest meadows in Shillely'. Incidentally, living in the neighbouring estate village of Carnew at that time were the ancestors of television personality Graham Norton (his family name was Walker), who had migrated from Greasbrough in the early eighteenth century, and continued to live in Carnew until the twentieth century. In the late eighteenth century, one of the Walker family was recorded as being an estate coppice keeper.

### The Irish estate woodlands

Thomas Watson-Wentworth also visited the estate woodlands and discussed their management with his agent and a woodward (a warden of a wood) from South Yorkshire who had travelled to Ireland especially for this purpose. By the beginning of the eighteenth century, the South Yorkshire estate contained twenty-eight coppice-with-standards woods (see below), covering nearly 900 acres, which were managed with great sophistication. The family exported their approach to woodland management in South Yorkshire to their Irish estates. By 1750, the Irish estate contained 2,356 acres (954 hectares) of coppice and scrub woods, of which 1,989 acres (805 hectares) were coppice woods proper, in thirty separate woods. They varied in size from 202 to 3 acres. Detailed accounts of their management have survived for the period 1707 to 1749, and a clear picture of management of underwood for a variety of local industries and constructional timber emerges.[4] It cannot be emphasised enough how important the estate woodlands in South Yorkshire and County Wicklow were to the income received by the estate. For example, in the period 1714–20, the gross average annual net income from the Shillelagh, Cashaw, Rathdrum and Kildare parts of the Irish estate was £7,805, of which almost exactly half came from rents and half from sales of timber, wood and bark.

During the first half of the eighteenth century, adjustments were made to the number and sizes of coppices, sometimes through planting but more usually by taking in adjacent scrub woods. Not only were existing coppices extended but completely new ones were created by enclosing good scrub woods. For example, one scrub wood, Nickson's Brow, was already a candidate in 1728 for conversion from scrub wood to coppice, a 1728 surveyor noting that 'if well reserved and fenced will make as good A Springe if not The Best in Shelelagh'. The coppices were mainly composed of oak, although birch was an important component of most woods. Other species included elm, hazel, holly, alder and willow.

**A view of the former Watson-Wentworth estate from the Kilcavan Gap across the Derry valley towards Tinahely, with the Wicklow Mountains in the background.**

The Irish coppice woods were managed as coppice-with-standards, like their South Yorkshire counterparts. In a coppice-with-standards, most trees were periodically cut down to ground level; they then grew back and were cut again, usually after twenty to twenty-five years. This process went on continually. Among the coppice growth, single-stemmed trees were allowed to grow on and on until they became mature trees. These were the standards. The coppice produced wood and the standards produced timber. From 1707 to 1749, coppice cycles varied from sixteen to thirty-three years. The standards were overwhelmingly oak, but ash, elm and alder were also mentioned. The most vital element in coppice management is protection of the coppice growth from grazing animals. The Watson-Wentworth Irish coppices were protected by ditches, i.e. ditched banks. In some places double ditches were constructed. The banks were planted with whitethorn (hawthorn) hedges. In some cases, there was a double hedge. Wood surveyors sent over from England sometimes recorded depredation of coppices through illegal browsing by farm animals. One surveyor in 1728 noted that part of one coppice had been 'Eaten as Bare as A Bowling Green'! Another problem was trespass and pilfering of wood, timber and bark. The surveyor from England and Abraham Nickson would have been at pains to point out how carefully the woods were protected and trespassers and thieves dealt with. In Abraham Nickson's account books for the period 1714 to 1720, there is a section devoted entirely to 'Trespasses in his Honour's Woods'.[5] During the seven-year period in question, Nickson recorded twenty-six cases of trespass, theft and the purchase of stolen items from his employer's coppice-with-standards woods. Among the crimes committed were the theft of small saplings, staves, cordwood (8-foot lengths of underwood used in making charcoal), cleft timber, carr timber (the material for making a two-wheeled cart), timber that was made into a chest, two tables, and several cases of 'filching' bark. He also recorded the fines imposed on the thieves and the payments he made to various estate employees and others who provided 'intelligence', and his own journeys around the county to provide evidence against people who had knowingly bought stolen wood and timber and who were 'bound over'.

Building timber was a very important product of these Irish woods in the first half of the eighteenth century. It was sold by the named piece and in undifferentiated lots. Named pieces included unworked wood, described as poles and saplings, and semi-finished and finished articles such as cleft spars, principals, purlins, beams, collar beams, hammer beams, rafters, laths, shingles, lintels, doorcases, clapboard and 'window stuff'. Named industrial items included helves, millshafts and timber for waterwheels. Timber was also provided for a substantial number of named building projects including Dublin Barracks, for which £1,423 was received in 1708–1709 (this must have been the famous Collins Barracks, now a museum, which was built from 1704 to 1710), and Dublin 'Colledge' in 1719 (the famous long room in the Old Library at Trinity College was built from 1712 to 1732).

In the first half of the eighteenth century, timber was also supplied for the construction of important buildings across the estate. These included courthouses at Athy, Carlow and Wicklow, repairs to market houses at Blessington and Newtown Mount Kennedy, new churches at Coolkenna, Donard, Inch and Kilcullen, church repairs at Ballymore, Baltinglass, Carnew, Clonegall, Donaghmoor, Hacketstown, Hollywood, Kilcommon,

Lymrick and Tullow, a new gaol at Carlow, five bark mills and a fulling mill. Timber, along with carpenters and joiners, was provided for building four 'school houses' from 1713 to 1718. Significantly, Thomas Watson-Wentworth had also built Barrow School in his home estate village of Wentworth in South Yorkshire in 1716. Fifteen pieces of timber were sold for making a bridge near Donard. The accounts reveal a great diversity of business with buyers great and small. Jostling with purchasers of many tons of building timber were customers like the one in 1715 who bought ten round poles for a dog house!

Lying within a reasonable distance from the Irish Sea coast, ship timber, like general building timber, was an important product of the standard trees of the Irish woods. Ship timber was sold squared, sawn and in the round. It was sold in the woods at timber yards, and delivered sometimes at the estate's expense, sometime at the buyer's. It was generally sold direct to shipbuilders, whose buyers came to the estate, but some went to dealers and some was carried to Wicklow 'to be laid on the Murrow for Sale'. The Murrough is the shingle beach that stretches northwards from the town.

Most of the ship timber went to Dublin and Wicklow, although a substantial proportion of that carried to Wicklow was then shipped to England. From 1707 to 1720, twenty-one shipbuilders and ship timber dealers were mentioned by name. Of the sixteen for whom a location was given, two, apparently dealers, were from within the estate itself, one was from Arklow, one was from Wexford, four were from Wicklow, four were from Dublin and five were from Whitehaven in Cumbria. There are several references in the accounts of timber for Whitehaven shipbuilders being taken by cart to Wicklow for dispatch across the Irish Sea.

Other important sources of income for the estate, through its careful management of its thirty coppice woods, were oak bark for leather tanning and cordwood for charcoal making. Bark for tanning was sold by the barrel. Once it was peeled, the bark was stooked to dry and then ground in water-powered bark mills, of which there were eight on the estate in the 1707–20 period. In 1713, when Thomas Watson-Wentworth was visiting the estate, there were sixteen different customers for bark. Dublin was the largest market for bark but besides being sold throughout County Wicklow, it was sold in towns as far as County Kildare, County Wexford and County Carlow. The market for cordwood for charcoal making was fairly small when Thomas Watson-Wentworth visited the Irish estates. The market at that time was entirely within Shillelagh, where the Chamney family had an ironworks (a furnace and a forge) and another tenant had a forge. But whether they produced building timber, ship timber, oak bark or charcoal, the Irish woods were a crucial element in the economy of Thomas Watson-Wentworth's Irish estate, and he was keenly interested in their management and protection.

**Journey's end**
By early October 1713, Thomas Watson-Wentworth was back in Dublin having spent time visiting his smaller properties in Wicklow Town, Newcastle and Rathdrum. He continued to have meetings with Abraham Nickson, who moved between Dublin and various places within the estate. Drawing up and signing leases, meeting those chief tenants who lived wholly or for part of the year in Dublin, and taking part in the social and cultural life of Dublin would have taken up much of Thomas Watson-Wentworth's time. It is interesting

**The wolf cub being shown to Thomas by Dennis Duiggen.** *Eric Leslie*

that during this period, Nickson arranged for his master to taste Ireland's unique drink and meet an animal long extinct in England. On 13 October, payment was made to a man who 'fetched a vessel of Usqebagh from Drogheda'. Usquebaugh is the Gaelic for 'water of life', in other words, Irish whiskey. And on 28 October, Nickson paid Dennis Duiggen for 'bringing ye Wolf whelp from Coolattin for his Honr'. Wolves had been extinct in England since the late fourteenth century and in Wales since the twelfth century. In Scotland, they persisted much longer and there are records of them as late as 1690 to 1700. The last Irish recorded sighting was in the mountains on the borders of the counties of Carlow and Wexford in 1780. The final record of Thomas's stay in Ireland was on 11 November 1713, when Nickson recorded that he was due 'to Imbarque for England'.

Although they were absentee landlords living a long distance from their Irish estates, the Watson-Wentworths and their successors, the Fitzwilliams, continued to set long leases with many subclauses, leading to the continued improvement of their properties. Almost a century after Thomas Watson-Wentworth's visit to his Irish estates, Edward Wakefield in his *An Account of Ireland, statistical and political* (1812) stated that 'Earl Fitzwilliam's Wicklow estate exhibited an appearance that would do honour to any part of Europe'. Praise indeed!

## Chapter 3

# THE 1ST MARQUIS OF ROCKINGHAM'S JOURNAL, 1723–50

O n his father's death in 1723, Thomas Watson-Wentworth, the future 1st Marquis of Rockingham, set out the details of his estate in a large vellum volume, 40 cm long and 30 cm wide (16 inches by 12 inches). This 'rent roll' book contains 130 leaves of vellum (fine parchment from the skin of a calf) with eighty-seven pages written on, the whole volume being fastened by two metal clasps. There

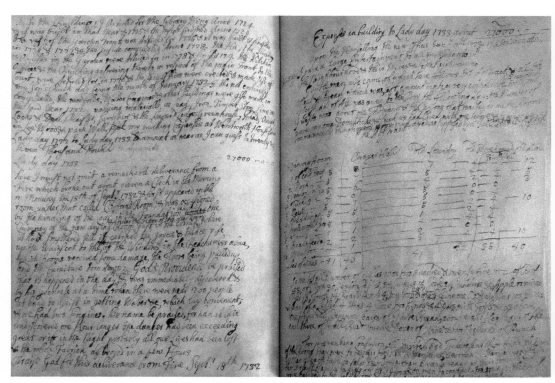

**The 1st Marquis of Rockingham's rent roll book.** *WWM A1273*

are also a number of loose sheets inside the volume. It is now item WWM A1273 in the Wentworth Woodhouse Muniments collection in Sheffield Archives. The volume seems to have originated as a record of manorial courts in 1654. It was then turned round and the details of Thomas Watson-Wentworth's estate begun at the other end. Important and interesting as the details of purchases, sales and rents on the estate are, the overriding interest of the volume lies in the fact that the future 1st Marquis also used the volume to record in his own hand what he called 'many remarks and observations', i.e. it was also his journal. His jottings extend from 1723 to almost the day he died in 1750. He gives details of his family, his building projects, the development of his park and garden, his hobbies and interests, and even wrote out in his own hand two detailed management plans for his South Yorkshire coppice woods. The volume, therefore, gives a fascinating insight into the life and concerns of an eighteenth-century aristocratic landowner.

### The man himself

Thomas Watson-Wentworth, the future 1st Marquis of Rockingham, was born in 1693 and died in 1750. He was the son of Thomas Watson, the third son of the 2nd Baron Rockingham, and his wife Anne, the sister of the 2nd Earl of Strafford. As already outlined in Chapter 2, the 2nd Earl of Strafford had died childless in 1695, and Thomas Watson inherited the Wentworth estates. The will specified that he change his name to Watson-Wentworth and reside at Wentworth. On Thomas Watson-Wentworth's death in 1723, the estates passed to his son, the future 1st Marquis.

Young Thomas, the future 1st Marquis, entered St John's College, Cambridge, in 1707 and was awarded an MA in 1708. In 1716, he married Mary, daughter of Daniel Finch, 2nd Earl of Nottingham and 6th Earl of Winchelsea. He was a strong supporter of the Hanoverian succession and was the organiser of Whig power in Yorkshire. He was MP for Malton from 1715 to 1727 and for the County of Yorkshire in 1727 to 1728. His support for the Whig cause and the suppression of the 1745 Jacobite rebellion brought him a succession of honours. In 1728, he was created Baron Wentworth of Malton, and in 1734, Baron of Harrowden, and

**Thomas Watson-Wentworth (1693–1750), 1st Marquis of Rockingham, from a painting by John Shackleton.** *Rotherham Archives and Local Studies*

Viscount Higham of Higham Ferrers, Northamptonshire, and Baron of Wath and Earl of Malton. In 1745, on the death of his cousin Thomas Watson, 3rd Earl of Rockingham, he succeeded to the barony of Rockingham (the earldom ceasing to exist). Finally, in 1746, he was created Marquis of Rockingham. He was Lord Lieutenant of the West Riding of Yorkshire from 1733 until his death in 1750. He was buried in York Minster. His widow died in 1761.

## Notes about his children

Thomas and Mary had ten children, five sons and five daughters. Only one son, the youngest, Charles, who became the 2nd Marquis, survived his father. For five of them – Anne (born 1722), Mary (born 1727), William (born 1728), Charlotte (born 1732) and Henrietta Alicia (born 1737) – he compiled a list not only giving their exact dates of birth but also their (mostly aristocratic) godparents. The other children to whom he refers are Thomas (born 1720) and Charles, the future 2nd Marquis of Rockingham.

On 9 January 1733, he wrote that he gave a large party to celebrate Thomas's thirteenth birthday and also the near completion of the Baroque mansion. This is described in detail in Chapter 10. But he later went on to describe his son Thomas's early death from 'the Small Pox at Leyden' on 14 August 1734. That date, 14 August, was not a lucky one for the family. Thomas also noted in his journal that:

> the same day was very remarkable to my present Eldest Son William. On 14 August he fell into the Bason in the Garden when no Body but a Boy was by, who providentially helped him out else he had probably been drowned being very young & on 14 August 1732 as he hastily shut a Door, a large Picture which hung over it fell down with such violence as to shatter the frame to pieces & by God's providence fell over the child so as he remained unhurt between the Door and the Picture.

William only survived until 1739, his father recording his early death thus: 'after a Feaverish illness of about a month's continuance dyed at Hampstead'. William's death and the earlier death of Thomas gave the future 1st Marquis pause for thought at the end of 1739:

> so that this Unfortunate Year when I lost my Dear Eldest Son William Lord Higham for whom I hoped to have prepared these Conveniencys [i.e. his new building projects at Wentworth Woodhouse] I had laid out in the whole as near as I could compute fifty six thousand pound – God - Preventt our being attached to the Honours Grandeur or State of the World above what we ought & Bless my now Dear & only son Charles to a long and Christian life to the enjoyment of these so as to be fit at leaving them to enjoy Everlasting Glory.

But six years later, he was to have another scare, during the Jacobite rebellion. The aim of the rebellion was the removal of the Protestant Hanoverian King George II from the throne and his replacement by the Roman Catholic James Edward Stuart, the

'Old Pretender', who lived in exile. The Pretender sent his 25-year-old son Charles Edward, Bonnie Prince Charlie, the Young Pretender, to represent him. In September 1745, the Young Pretender's army captured Edinburgh, defeated the English army at Prestonpans, east of Edinburgh, and invaded England. Subsequently they advanced as far south as Derby by early December. In the face of advancing English troops under the Duke of Cumberland, they decided to retreat and were back in Carlisle by late December. They then retreated back into Scotland. The rebellion came to an end with their defeat at the Battle of Culloden in April 1746 by the English and German army under the Duke ('Butcher') of Cumberland. The Young Pretender escaped.

Hoober Stand was completed in 1748. This 'Pyramidal building', as he called it in his journal, was erected by the 1st Marquis of Rockingham in honour of King George II and the suppression of the rebellion. That's one explanation of the building of Hoober Stand: the loyalty of the 1st Marquis to his king. This is announced very plainly in a plaque above the door:

> 1748
> This Pyramidal Building was Erected
> By his Majestys most Dutifull Subject
> THOMAS Marquess of Rockingham, etc
> In Grateful Respect to the Preserver of our
> Religion
> Laws and Libertys
> KING GEORGE The second
> Who by the blessing of God having Subdued a
> Most Unnatural Rebellion
> In Britain Anno 1746
> Maintains the Balance of Power and Settles
> A just and Honourable peace in Europe
> 1748

But there may be more to it than that, because the 1st Marquis's only surviving son, Charles, who would succeed him, had run off to join the Duke of Cumberland and his army, who were pursuing the retreating Jacobites. The future 1st Marquis would no doubt be worried stiff that the future 2nd Marquis might also lose his life.

What is staggering is that Charles was only 15 when he went off secretly to join the Duke of Cumberland. But he was also a colonel in his father's volunteer army, which had been recruited to fight the Jacobites. Apparently, he was out hunting near Wakefield on 18 December 1745 when he claimed he was hungry and went back to the town. There he armed himself with three pistols and a sword, and secretly rode northwards to join the Duke. He rode via Bradford, Skipton, Settle and Kendal, arriving in Carlisle on 22 December. The Duke of Cumberland took good care of him and kept him away from any skirmishes with the Jacobites. Meanwhile, his father had sent out search parties to look for him. In the end he was returned home safely, but by then he had gone up in everybody's estimation, even the royal family's, for his patriotism and bravery.

**Hoober Stand.**

So, Hoober Stand was not only built in honour of King George II but also probably in relief at the safe return from the battlefront of the future 2nd Marquis, who, it must be remembered, became Prime Minister twice.

## His house building projects

In 1724, the future 1st Marquis started building the west-facing Baroque mansion. But before he had finished building and furnishing it, in 1734, he began to erect another, bigger house in the Palladian style, facing east. It is this latter mansion, which was not completed until after his death in 1750, that people will be most familiar with today.

He meticulously recorded progress, setbacks and expenditure on his building projects in his journal, although interestingly, he fails to mention his architects/builders Ralph Tunnicliffe and Henry Flitcroft. He noted that, in 1724, he had 'articled for the Library wing' and that this had been 'built in 1725 and furnished inside in 1726'. By 'articled' he meant that he had come to an agreement with his architects/builders. He went on to record that he had 'articled' for the 'rest of the Garden front in 1725', which had been built in 1726 and 1727, and the inside finished in 1728. The kitchen was articled for in 1730 and made use of in 1733. He computed that his outlay on building work from 1722 to 1733 was more than £27,000.

By the spring of 1736, building expenditure had risen to more than £36,000 and included the construction of part of the new front '7 windows in length'. On 28 June 1736, he recorded that 'Prayers were said in the New Chappel for the first time'. In 1737 he noted that the new parlour and drawing room were finished, furnished and in use, and the great hall (i.e. what is now called the Pillared Hall) and portico begun. By 1738, the great hall was built and covered and the 'supping room' finished. In 1739, the 'great porticoe' of the east (Palladian) front was finished. He said of this that 'considering the Size of the stones & the Quantity of Carving, etc [it] was the greatest piece of building I had ever done in one Year'. By the spring of 1739, his building expenditure at Wentworth had risen to £56,000, and by 1744, by which time he was buying Cumberland slate for the main roof, it was £74,000.

By 1748 he was able to record that there was 'nothing but Furnishing, Finishing and Levelling' to be done. At the end of the year his total building expenses had reached an astonishing £86,000, including £3,500 for 'Statues bought ... by Ld Malton (the future 2nd Marquis) at Rome and other places'. These purchases had taken place during the future 2nd Marquis's 'Grand Tour'. By the time he died in 1750, the building expenses had reached £90,000.

Amongst the recitation of building achievements and monetary outlay he described a fire that occurred during the morning of 18 November 1732. Having described how it was thought to have started by some burning coal having set light to floor joists, which then spread and caused damage to some bedrooms, he goes on to say:

> God's Providence be praised that it happened in the daytime & was immediately discovered & by his Goodness at a time when there were near 200 people at hand to assist in getting Water etc, which lay convenient, & we had two Engines, his name be praised, for had it lain undiscovered

**The Van Dyck Room in 1924, so called because of the portraits by that artist on the walls. This room was once called the State Drawing Room. The painting on the left is Thomas, 1st Earl of Strafford.** *Country Life Picture Library*

one Hour longer the danger had been exceeding great or if in the Night probably all our Lives had been lost & the whole Fabrick destroyed in a few Hours. Praise God for his deliverance from Fire Septr18th 1732.

Besides his house building, he gives details of the work he was doing on redesigning and enlarging his park and gardens, including the building of monuments, the creation of a serpentine lake and the creation of a menagerie, and these projects are covered in Chapter 6.

By the 1740s he had another obsession: growing pineapples. It is believed the first pineapple to be grown in England was in the 1670s when gardener John Rose presented one to King Charles II. But pineapple growing on any scale did not begin until the 1720s, and by the 1730s large landowners were said to be in the grip of 'Pineapple Fever'. They were first sunk into 'tan pits', which were brick-lined pits covered with glass. The pineapples were grown in tan bark (disused oak bark from leather tanneries), which kept the roots at a temperature of 75–85 degrees Fahrenheit. Eventually, specialised houses called 'pineries' were constructed that contained tan pits and beds warmed by warm-air flues and later by water boilers. The future 1st Marquis started growing pineapples in 1737, stating that they were then 'very scarce in England'. By the 1740s, he was famed for growing pineapples. In 1740, he recorded in his journal that he had got their cultivation to 'great perfection'. He produced one that weighed 3½ lb and was 20 inches from top to bottom and 16 inches around its widest part. In 1745, he says some were ripe as early as 24 March and he had them transported to London 'for an Entertainment I made' at which the Duke of Richmond, the Earl of Lincoln, Earl Fitzwilliam and Lord Harcourt were present. He noted that by the second week in June that year he had cut more than 200, sometimes as many as sixteen per day. He also noted that he had cut several hundred in 1747.

**His estate**

He listed all his properties as they stood in 1723, itemised all the rents and gave an overall evaluation for the entire estate. The rents from South Yorkshire amounted to £4,448, for Malton in the North Riding it was £2,020, for Northamptonshire and other places in the Midlands it was £3,050, and for Ireland £6,446, making a grand total of nearly £16,000. In addition he reckoned he could expect an annual income of about £1,000 from his coppice woods in England and Ireland. He also put the value of his timber trees on his English and Irish properties at £25,000. In one of his last entries in 1748 he put his annual rental income at £19,000.

Not only did the future 1st Marquis itemise all the properties belonging to the estate, he also gave details of purchases and sales. It is clear that, like his father before him and his son who would follow him, he had a four-pronged attitude to property owning: to enlarge the whole estate, to consolidate the home estate in South Yorkshire, to maximise estate income, and to ensure a place on the country's political stage through the acquisition of 'rotten boroughs'.

When his father died in 1723, the future 1st Marquis inherited a vast estate comprising almost 11,000 acres (4,452 hectares) in South Yorkshire, 90,000 acres (36,422 hectares) in Ireland and several thousand acres in the Midlands, mainly in Northamptonshire. From 1723 to his death in 1750, he made twenty-four purchases in South Yorkshire, adding a further 2,116 acres (856 hectares). In South Yorkshire, his purchases were either in Wentworth itself or in townships and parishes to the north and east; none to the south and west. This geographical anomaly was because of the already existing large estates to the south (belonging to the Duke of Norfolk) and to the west (belonging to the Wortley family and the Earls of Strafford of the second creation at Wentworth Castle), which blocked any expansion in those two directions. Only one purchase – Hallfield House at Bradfield (used as a hunting lodge) and its surrounding farmland, which was bought by the future 1st Marquis's father in 1708, took place in the eighteenth century. He bought land from yeoman farmers, indebted minor gentry and from large landowners who held detached properties there. His purchases had two ambitions: first, to fill in gaps and so consolidate his holdings, and secondly, to expand his estate outwards. To fill gaps, no purchase was too small. For example, in 1725 he bought one acre of land in Barrow Field in Wentworth for £11; in 1735, he bought a little close in Greasbrough covering just over 1½ acres in Westhill Field for £30; and in the same year he bought a piece of land also in Greasbrough, covering just 25 perches (one-eighth of an acre) for just £3. He also recorded swapping small pieces of land to consolidate his holdings. In contrast to these small purchases and exchanges he also purchased land in large blocks of several hundred acres. Some of these large South Yorkshire purchases would have a double significance over the next two centuries: they lay above the rich Middle Coal Measures and therefore would not only provide rental income from farms but also income from colliery development, either directly by the Wentworth family or from royalties from private coal mining companies who were given permission to develop collieries. For example, in 1750, the year he died, he purchased Viscount Galway's estate, which lay mainly in Hoyland Nether, covered 337 acres (136 hectares) and was located over the outcrop of the 9-foot thick Barnsley coal seam. The Galway estate also contained 60 acres (24 hectares) of woodland, which would be added to 876 acres (355 hectares) of coppice-with-standards that already brought a considerable income to the South Yorkshire estate. And to round off his continuous interest in the expansion of his woodland resources, his last purchase, in 1750, was Edlington Woods, near Doncaster, covering 400 acres (162 hectares), from a landowner whose main estate was in County Durham.

As well as recording details of his land purchases in South Yorkshire, the future 1st Marquis also wrote out in his own hand two detailed coppice wood management schemes, the first covering the period from 1727 to 1748, and the second from 1749 to 1770, i.e. both with coppice cycles of twenty-one years. Within each acre of coppice he emphasised that there should be left standing five mature timber trees ('black barks') and seventy young timber trees ('weavers'). The 1727 scheme was what he called 'A Scheme for making a yearly considerable Profit of the Spring Woods in Yorkshire'. The 1749 scheme was called 'A Scheme for a Regular Fall of Wood for 21 years … amounting to about nine Hundred acres', i.e. about 42 acres (17 hectares) a year. Thirty-one woods were involved, including two very large ones that were compartmented: the 350-acre (142-hectare) Tinsley Park in nine separate compartments, and the 126-acre (51-hectare) Westwood in three separate compartments. The scheme ends with the phrase '& so begin the Circle again'. He specifically excluded Scholes Coppice, which had by then been made part of the park. What is interesting is that many of the woods mentioned in the 1727 and 1749 schemes are still features of the twenty-first-century landscape, including King's Wood and Simon Wood at Elsecar, Luke Spring at Street, Bassingthorpe Spring at Greasbrough, Westwood at Tankersley, Thorncliffe Wood at Chapeltown, and Rainborough Park and Giles Wood at Brampton.

Besides his enormous properties in Ireland and his expanding South Yorkshire estate, the future 1st Marquis had properties in Malton in North Yorkshire, in the Midlands (mainly Northamptonshire), and in London, all of which he refers to in his journal. The borough of Malton was purchased by his father, Thomas Watson-Wentworth, in 1713, and much of the town is still owned by the future 1st Marquis's descendants. Among important buildings in the town associated with the 1st Marquis are the Talbot Hotel, which he acquired in 1740 and was at first used as a hunting lodge, and the town hall, the building of which he commissioned in 1749, the year before his death. Malton was a 'rotten borough' where, as the major landowner, he or his representative could represent the town in Parliament. As noted above, he was MP for Malton from 1715 to 1727. In his journal he noted the yearly rents he got from property in the town and that he had bought land 'at or near Malton The Navigation included'. This last reference is related to the funding of work to make the river Derwent navigable to Malton, work that was completed by his son, the 2nd Marquis.

At various times in the eighteenth century, the Watson-Wentworths also owned properties in six Midland counties: Leicestershire, Rutland, Warwickshire, Huntingdonshire, Bedfordshire and Northamptonshire. The future 1st Marquis's rent roll of 1723 lists property at Tidmington in Warwickshire, Greetham in Rutland, Yaxley in Huntingdonshire and Dadlington and Shenton in Leicestershire, but these had almost all been disposed of by the end of the 1730s. His father, Thomas Watson-Wentworth the elder, also sold a property at Gumley in Leicestershire in 1714. The properties in Leicestershire, Rutland, Warwickshire, Huntingdonshire and Bedfordshire came into the family through inheritance or purchase, and their sale had the effect of concentrating their landed interests in the Midlands into a small area in eastern Northamptonshire, where there were two separate and very different estates.

The first of these was the Harrowden estate, centred on Harrowden Hall in Great Harrowden parish and extending into the neighbouring parishes of Little Harrowden and Orlingbury, and a number of exclaves of varying size including Finedon, Irthlingborough and Mears Ashby. Of the 1,930 acres in the three adjacent parishes of Great Harrowden, Little Harrowden and Orlingbury, all but about 350 acres were in Great Harrrowden, where, according to John Bridges in *The History and Antiquities of Northamptonshire*,[1] Thomas Watson-Wentworth the elder owned 'the whole lordship excepting one small meadow'. In Orlingbury, the Watson-Wentworth property comprised the 222-acre Withmale Park Farm and the 83-acre Withmale Park Wood (which in his 1749 coppice wood plan he specifically states that it should not be coppiced, even though it is not a South Yorkshire wood!). The wood still survives and is a Site of Special Scientific Interest (SSSI) because it contains the rare ancient woodland indicator species Herb Paris and four species of orchids. The Harrowden estate also included the tithes of Great and Little Harrowden and the advowsons of the Harrowdens and Irthlingborough. The rental income from the Northamptonshire estates was substantial. On Lady Day 1750, for example, the Great and Little Harrowden rents amounted to £665-18s-8d. Lady Day was 25 March. Rents were usually paid twice a year, on Lady Day and at Michaelmas.[2]

The Harrowden properties were acquired from one vendor, the 4th Earl of Banbury, but the purchase was a complicated one and took nine years to complete. The Banbury properties had been inherited by Charles Knowles (or Knolles or Knollys), 4th Earl of Banbury, in 1684 and the agreement to sell to Thomas Watson-Wentworth was dated 1693, just two years before Thomas Watson-Wentworth succeeded to the estates of his uncle, the 2nd Earl of Strafford. The purchase is said to have been finalised in 1695.

The agreed purchase price was £29,175-18s-2d. The purchase price included £12,800 of debts that Thomas Watson-Wentworth agreed to pay off. The vendor has been described as a debt-ridden 'rake, dissolute and riotous' who among other things had killed his brother-in-law in a duel.

According to Bridges in his *The History and Antiquities of Northamptonshire*, Harrowden Hall was 'new built by Mr Wentworth', but the *Victoria County History of Northamptonshire*[3] says that 'the present hall appears to have been begun ... about 1687 ... but was probably renovated and perhaps enlarged by Thomas Watson-Wentworth after his purchase of the property'. It also states that the date 1712 is on the spout heads of the house. In his journal, the future 1st Marquis noted that in 1723, 'Great Harrowden House, Gardens and Park & Demesnes' were 'in the Occupation of the Honble Mrs Wentworth' (his mother).

The second Northamptonshire estate was centred on Higham Ferrers (635 acres), with small properties in five surrounding villages. They were largely purchased from Louis, 2nd Earl of Feversham, by Thomas Watson-Wentworth, with later purchases by his son, in the early 1730s. This was another 'rotten borough'. Thomas Watson-Wentworth was elected MP for Higham Ferrers at the general elections of 1703, 1705, 1708 and 1710, and then again 1722.

Lastly, he noted that he had bought a house in Grosvenor Square in London in 1741. This was No. 4 Grosvenor Square, and it remained the family's main London base until it was sold by the 7th Earl Fitzwilliam early last century. It is now the Italian Embassy.

**Conclusion**

It is unusual to be able to put together a coherent study of one large country estate at one period in time from just one source, and this is what makes the 1st Marquis's rent roll-cum-journal so fascinating. The combined force of the formal rental entries and his observations and jottings make this a unique document and provides a real insight into his preoccupations – personal, political and dynastic. But it is his estate that lies at the centre of his concerns. In 1750, the year of his death, he wrote to his son, the future 2nd Marquis: 'If you lay out your money in improving your seat, land, gardens, etc, you beautifye the country and do the work ordered by God himself.'

*Chapter 4*

# THE 2ND MARQUIS OF ROCKINGHAM AND THE AMERICAN COLONIES

Wentworth Woodhouse was a political and economic powerhouse, and Rockingham's associates did much to forge modern Britain and champion political values still relevant today.[1]

In his TV programme about Wentworth Woodhouse, broadcast in 2011, the architectural historian Dan Cruickshank explained the importance of the estate in the eighteenth century. The 2nd Marquis of Rockingham was the leader of the most important section of the Whig Party from 1765 to 1782, years in which he controlled the representation of Yorkshire in the House of Commons, and was Lord Lieutenant of the West Riding, which meant that he controlled the militia. This was a time when British politics was turned upside down by the accession of George III and the American Revolution; but, although Rockingham became Prime Minister twice, his time in power was brief. For most of his political career, he was in opposition to King George III's governments. As Prime Minister from 1765 to 1766, he repealed the Stamp Act (which had provoked serious unrest in the Thirteen American Colonies) and consistently argued in favour of reconciliation with the Americans, but he failed to persuade a majority of the House of Commons to his way of thinking. As a result, there was a long and bloody war. When he became Prime Minister once more in 1782, it was on condition that George III recognised American independence, but he died before peace could be negotiated.

### Rockingham's politics

What motivated Rockingham to enter politics? To a large extent, it was expected of him, but in his groundbreaking work *The Structure of Politics at the Accession of George III* (1930), Sir Lewis Namier cynically wrote that 'Men went into politics to make a figure; and no more dreamt of a seat in Parliament in order to benefit humanity than a child dreams of a birthday cake in order that others may eat it.' However, Rockingham was one of the richest men in Britain, and really did not need the financial rewards of office. In addition, he had a seat in the House of Lords from 1751 and did not need to stand for election to the House of Commons thereafter. Moreover, his career is not one to provide food for the cynics. He often acted against his own self-interest, in championing an unpopular cause.

**Statue of the 2nd Marquis of Rockingham in the Mausoleum.**

Like his father, the 2nd Marquis was a pillar of the Whig establishment but, unlike his father, he had serious differences of opinion with the monarch. Why? In 1760, George II had died and was succeeded by his young grandson, George III. The new sovereign wanted to change the old ways of doing things, by breaking the Whig stranglehold on office. Accordingly, he appointed his friend and mentor Lord Bute as Prime Minister, and the old guard of Whigs, who had held office ever since George I of Hanover came to the throne in 1715, were excluded from power. Rockingham resigned his post of Lord of the Bedchamber and in turn George III removed him from his offices of Lord Lieutenant of the West Riding of Yorkshire, Lord Lieutenant of the City and County of York, and Vice-Admiral of the North. The Whigs came to think that George was trying to ape the Stuarts, and was dreaming of an absolute monarchy. In their view, the power of the Crown had now increased, was still increasing and ought to be curtailed once more. On the other hand, the King and his 'friends' thought that there had been 'a wicked cornering of power' by the King's ministers during the previous reign, and that the monarch was fully entitled to exercise his constitutional right to choose his own ministers as he saw fit.[2]

Who was right? Politicians were bitterly divided by the issue at the time and ultimately, two schools of historiography arose – the Whig and the Tory. The historian can only seek to explain and not be partisan, but during the 1760s and 1770s, Rockingham's name became closely associated with that of his secretary, Edmund Burke, who justified his master's actions in terms of a new definition of 'party'. Previously, the word had been synonymous with 'faction', but Burke defined it as 'a body of men united for promoting by their joint endeavours the national interest upon some particular principle in which they are all agreed', which is pretty much how we see things today. At the time it was seen as 'humbug' by the Tories. Rockingham became the leader, for the first time, of the new Whigs, though the group lacked many of the characteristics of a modern political party.

### The dispute with America

George III has had a particularly bad press in America, where he is generally regarded as a tyrant, but at the time there was little difference of opinion between the King and the majority of MPs at Westminster about American issues. British politicians of all descriptions tended to think that it was the first duty of the colonists to obey the wishes of His Majesty and his ministers, but there were two areas where a significant number of colonists were not prepared to comply with their directives. These related to: the movement of American settlers to the west of the Appalachian Mountains and the enforcement of the British 'Proclamation Line', which sought to put a limit to that expansion; and the right of the Westminster Parliament to regulate American trade and tax the Thirteen Colonies (which had traditionally been allowed to manage their own affairs, and raise their own taxes).

As to the last of these issues, expenditure incurred during the Seven Years' War of 1756–63 had created a large deficit in the British budget, which any government would have tried to reduce. In 1765, the administration headed by George Grenville introduced a Stamp Act, imposing a tax on all documents in the Thirteen Colonies, including newspapers (one of the few ways in those days of expressing dissent). This was designed to make the Americans pay more for their own defence – a not unreasonable demand from the British point of view, but it produced immediate resistance in America, where the famous rallying cry of 'no taxation without representation' was raised. This was followed by radical action. In New York, the Stamp Act was reprinted and sold in the streets as 'England's folly and America's ruin'. In Philadelphia, the guns of Royal Artillery pieces were spiked. In Boston, the flags of the vessels in harbour were flown at half-mast. The American 'Sons of Liberty' used public demonstrations, boycotts, violence and threats of violence to ensure that the new tax could not be collected, and a Stamp Act Congress that convened in New York City in October 1765 decided on a non-importation agreement – the first step in creating unity between the Thirteen Colonies, which had previously been much divided, both by geography and in sentiment. Meanwhile, the Stamp Act was also unpopular in Britain for economic reasons. Historians debate nowadays whether it really led to a recession, but it is clear that many people at the time thought that it did.

The 2nd Marquis of Rockingham had a number of ways of keeping in touch with American affairs. He was a sociable man who knew many landowners, but also manufacturers involved in the woollen, iron and coal trades in the West Riding of Yorkshire, as well as merchants in the ports and industrial areas of England who traded with America,[3] and he also got to know several prominent Americans. In particular, he was provided with information by John Wentworth of New Hampshire, the nephew of the governor of that province from 1741 to 1766; Barlow Trecothick, who had been brought up in Massachusetts but settled in London, where he became a merchant and an MP for the City; and Benjamin Franklin, traditionally one of the Founding Fathers of the USA (though he never became president). Franklin spent the best part of twenty years in England from the 1750s to the 1770s, and represented Pennsylvania, Massachusetts, New York and Georgia at Whitehall.

Rockingham was therefore familiar with the American point of view, and he sympathised with the concerns of American and British merchants who engaged in transatlantic trade. In order to reach a more informed decision as to how to proceed, he even commissioned a report from John Wentworth on American affairs in general, and in particular, on the effects of the Stamp Act on trade, but it should be stressed that his position was always a conservative one. He was no rebel, or republican, and he did not want any fundamental change in the relationship between the mother country and her colonies. However, he did conclude that it would have been better to leave the Americans alone, with the freedom to handle their own affairs, and he accurately predicted that the Stamp Act would prove to be a terrible and fateful mistake.

### The first Rockingham administration, 1765–66

The traditional view is that Rockingham assumed office as Prime Minister in July 1765, specifically pledged to repeal the Stamp Act, and that is certainly what his first administration is most famous for. The matter was debated intensively by Parliament, but the Rockingham Whigs assembled an impressive amount of evidence in support of repeal and they had the better of the argument. Barlow Trecothick and Benjamin Franklin gave evidence to the House of Commons, and Rockingham and his associates were very successful in managing Parliament, as well as in organising petitions in favour of their proposed course of action.

In the event, the Stamp Act was repealed by a large majority – 275 votes to 167 – but it is important to note that many MPs were vigorously opposed, and indeed regarded repeal as a craven surrender to the threat of armed force. Furthermore, Rockingham was only able to achieve repeal by enacting a Declaratory Act at the same time, stating that Westminster retained the right to legislate for the Colonies in all matters. In Rockingham's view, this right should never be used, but the fact was that the principle of the ultimate sovereignty of the Westminster Parliament (as opposed to the personal view of the monarch) was now enshrined in law, and Rockingham could not gainsay it. The Declaratory Act therefore undid part of the good work that the repeal of the Stamp Act had aimed to achieve in terms of bringing about a genuine reconciliation between Britain and the Colonies.

Rockingham lost office after only one year, but not before he had chance to appoint John Wentworth as Governor of New Hampshire and Surveyor General of His Majesty's Forests in North America, positions that the American continued to hold until 1775. Before leaving England to take up his new posts, John Wentworth spent some time in Yorkshire, though at Bretton Hall, not Wentworth Woodhouse.

As already noted, the repeal of the Stamp Act did not succeed in its objective of restoring harmony with the Americans, but it was popular for a time on both sides of the Atlantic because it did restore economic prosperity. According to Albemarle, the editor of the Marquis's correspondence, a deputation of London merchants waited upon Rockingham when he ceased to hold office and set out for Yorkshire. They presented him with an address, in which they expressed their gratitude. On his entry into York, he was attended by nearly 200 gentlemen, and on the next day, an address was presented to him by the magistrates and merchants of Leeds. Similar events took place in York, Halifax, Kingston upon Hull and Wakefield. It should also be noted that, according to Dr Marjorie Bloy, the repeal of the Stamp Act was intended to be merely the first stage of a programme that might have set Anglo-American relations, and imperial affairs in general, on an entirely new course: she considers it possible that '[Rockingham's] plan would probably have formed a secure and lasting foundation for continued Anglo-American friendship within the colonial context.'[4]

As it turned out, of course, in 1766 the Whigs entered a long period of opposition, during which they convinced themselves that they had been double-crossed. They constructed an elaborate theory that George III had never really supported their leader as Prime Minister and had instead presided over a parallel cabinet, composed of the King's friends and cronies, while constantly looking for an opportunity to oust the Whigs from the seat of power.

Nevertheless, in America, the repeal was the basis of Rockingham's enduring popularity with Loyalists, at least in some areas. Rockingham County in Virginia was formed in 1778. Rockingham City, the county seat of Richmond County, North Carolina, was named in 1784, while Rockingham County in the same province was formed in 1785. In New Hampshire, Governor John Wentworth created several new counties in 1769 – named after Rockingham himself, Grafton (one of the secretaries of state in his administration), Hillsborough (a secretary of state in the administration that followed), and Strafford (possibly Rockingham's cousin, the 2nd Earl of the 2nd creation, though he was Catholic, Tory and a Jacobite!). In addition, Wentworth House, Portsmouth, New Hampshire, was named after Governor John Wentworth, and Francestown and Deering, towns in Hillsborough County, were named after the latter's new wife.

## The American War of Independence, 1776–83

The Rockingham Whigs stayed out of office from 1766 to 1782. The Marquis reckoned there were about 170 MPs who were sympathetic to his point of view, but he could never quite pull off a return to government; indeed, his party now became known as the *enfants perdus* – the lost children – of politics. They fought the general elections of 1768, 1774 and 1780, but did not improve their position materially. Rockingham was in the fortunate position of not needing the rewards of office and he was able to endure the long absence from power with equanimity, having many other interests, but some of the Whigs became demoralised and even thought of giving up politics altogether.

Meanwhile, what of America? After Rockingham lost office, Pitt the Elder became Prime Minister again as Earl of Chatham (having previously held that office during the Seven Years' War), but it was Chancellor of the Exchequer Charles Townsend who now made a second attempt to tax the American colonists, this time by means of customs duties. These were fiercely resisted, as the Stamp Act had been, and the majority were repealed, but in a third and final attempt to make the Americans come to heel, Lord North's government then enacted the Tea Act of 1773, and notoriously this provoked the Boston Tea Party in Massachusetts. That in turn led to further escalation of the conflict, provoking the British Government into enacting the so-called 'Intolerable' Acts, aimed at coercion. Clashes between British troops and colonial militias resulted. A Royal Proclamation of August 1775 announced that America was 'in a state of open and avowed rebellion', and ultimately led to the American Declaration of Independence on 4 July the following year. It is well known that this contains a ringing denouncement of George III, concluding with the famous line: 'A Prince, whose character is thus marked by every act which may define a Tyrant, is unfit to be the ruler of a free people.' It is less well known that it also criticises the Westminster Parliament:

> Nor have we been wanting in attentions to our British brethren. We have warned them from time to time of attempts by their legislature to extend an unwarrantable jurisdiction over us. We have reminded them of the circumstances of our emigration and settlement here. We have appealed to their native justice and magnanimity; and we have conjured them by the ties of common kindred to disavow these usurpations, which would inevitably interrupt our connections and correspondence. They too have been deaf to the voice of justice and of consanguinity.

Rockingham's line on American taxation had been fleshed out by Edmund Burke, in his *Present State of the Nation* (1768), which argued that the right to legislate for the Colonies, set out in the Declaratory Act of 1766, should be used prudently, and not exercised in such a way as to vex the colonists. And they were not alone in being unwilling to coerce the colonists. The Marquis's friend Admiral Keppel at first refused a much-coveted command in the Royal Navy because it would involve fighting the colonists, and his fellow Yorkshireman, Thomas Earl of Effingham, responded to the Boston Tea Party by building Boston Castle in Rotherham, where he decreed that 'no tea should ever be drunk'. More importantly, he resigned his commission in the Army rather than fight the Americans. However, none of these men approved of armed resistance, let alone the establishment of a republic.

**Boston Castle in Rotherham, built for the Earl of Effingham in 1773 as a hunting lodge and named Boston Castle to commemorate the Boston Tea Party.** *Guest, 1879*

On the other side of the account, the power of patriotic solidarity was such that support for the Rockingham Whigs in Parliament plummeted when fighting broke out, and the war was initially popular with some. 'The merchants', wrote Burke, 'begin to snuff the cadaverous *haut gout* [strong smell] of lucrative war: the freighting business never was so lively, on account of the prodigious taking up for transport service; great orders for provisions of all kinds, new clothing for the troops, put life into the woollen manufactures.' Meanwhile, country gentlemen were deluded by the ministerial assurance that American taxation would relieve them of part of the land tax, and many people were pleased at the prospect of transferring a portion of their burdens to other shoulders. The fighting itself led to a polarisation of opinion. On the Tory side, Dr Johnson expressed a common British view that the Americans were hypocrites when he asked, 'How is it that we hear the loudest yelps for liberty amongst the drivers of Negroes?' Lastly, many British MPs blamed the Marquis and his friends for the crisis, taking the view that the repeal of the Stamp Act was a form of appeasement, which had only served to encourage the Americans to further aggression.

The war itself went very badly from the British point of view, and early in 1778, France signed a treaty of alliance with the United States and Spain, and the Dutch Republic also joined in on the American side, while Britain remained friendless. This is not the place to include details of the fighting, but it is important to note that, in 1779, there was a real danger that Britain herself would be invaded, and as Lord Lieutenant and commander of the West Riding militia, Rockingham was actively involved in defending Hull against the attack of the American privateer John Paul Jones. He deployed several cannon there, which incidentally were made in Walker's forges in Rotherham.

The only victory scored by the Whigs in the late 1770s was a legal one. In 1778, Rockingham's friend and associate Admiral Keppel was tried for desertion after the battle of Ushant. Rockingham suspected that the prosecution was politically motivated. The Admiral's acquittal was the occasion for a national celebration. (See Chapter 5.)

## The second Rockingham administration, of 1782

After Lord Cornwallis surrendered an entire British army to George Washington in October 1781, the House of Commons voted to end the American War, and Rockingham saw the King. His policy was not to accept office as Prime Minister unless George III agreed to his choice of ministers and his choice of policies, including no veto on the independence of the Colonies, and some measure of parliamentary reform. Historians disagree as to whether the King really agreed to these terms, but, at any rate, Rockingham duly became Prime Minister. However, the new administration was built on shaky foundations. It had equal numbers of Rockingham and Shelburne supporters. William Petty, 2nd Earl of Shelburne, was a Whig politician who became Prime Minister after the death of the 2nd Marquis. The final member was a royal observer whose first loyalty was to George III rather than to any politician or political party.

In addition, Rockingham died after only fourteen weeks in office, and this makes it difficult to assess his place in history. Notably, the Treaties of Paris, by which Britain recognised the independence of the new American states and returned Florida to Spain, were signed later, in 1782 and 1783, after his death. We are therefore left to wonder what would have happened if Rockingham had lived longer, or been a more skilful politician. Would there ever have been a USA? Would the colonists have settled for less than full independence if the British negotiators had taken a harder line? Or was it inevitable that the Colonies would go their own way, given that the option of 'dominion status' within the Empire had yet to be devised?

No one doubts that on a personal level, Rockingham was a likeable and sociable man who had the ability to 'get on', even with those who disagreed with him. He was also generous – responding favourably, for example, to many requests for financial assistance from dispossessed Loyalists in America. But contemporaries were divided, often on party lines, as to his abilities and achievements as a politician. Horace Walpole, who had always deprecated the Marquis, now wrote that he 'triumphed without the shadow of compromise of any sort [and] deserves all praise and all support'. The obituary in the *Gentleman's Magazine* stated that Rockingham's death had 'deprived the country of his services just when their consequence and value was beginning to be felt', but the truth is that the Marquis was, by and large, loved by Whigs and hated by Tories. The intense hostility felt by some is reflected in the scatological cartoon by Gillray of 21 May 1782, entitled *Evacuation before Resignation*.

Historians have also been divided. J.B. Owen wrote that in the mid-1760s, Rockingham was 'A shockingly poor speaker, an inept politician, dedicated more to the race-track than the Cabinet board with no clear ideas of importance on any political issue'. On the charge of ineptitude, Rockingham's first cabinet in 1765 was said to be 'a mere lute-string administration, pretty summer wear which will never survive the winter', while Owen even accused him of putting himself in a minority in his own cabinet in 1782. From the British point of view, Rockingham is also accused of being half-hearted about parliamentary reform, and it is true that he disliked John Wilkes's brand of Radicalism, just as he opposed the moderate proposals put forward by the Yorkshire reformer Christopher Wyvill. From the American perspective, it is said that Rockingham's support for the American cause was only half-hearted, but this criticism totally ignores the realities of British politics, as well as the importance of simple patriotism.

The problem posed by the Thirteen Colonies was essentially insoluble. Rockingham sympathised with the Americans when it came to the question of taxation, direct and indirect, but he also believed in the supremacy of the Westminster Parliament. The truth is that over many decades, the Americans had grown used to governing themselves and had come to resent any interference by Westminster and 'Whitehall'. Eventually, coercive measures led them to reject the sovereignty of the British Parliament altogether, along with that of the Crown. Accordingly, it is doubtful if the Marquis would have been able to achieve any different outcome, even if he had enjoyed better health, or lived longer, and even if he had been a more skilful and successful parliamentarian.

*Chapter 5*

# KEPPEL AND HIS COLUMN

A dmiral Augustus Keppel (1725–86) was court-martialled, on board HMS *Britannia*, in Portsmouth Harbour, from Thursday, 8 January to Thursday, 11 February 1779. It was alleged that he had been guilty of five separate acts of misconduct and neglect during the Battle of Ushant the previous year. After two days of manoeuvring and skirmishing off the coast of Brittany, the Royal Navy had withdrawn to English waters without further engaging the enemy.

**Keppel's Column.**

The court martial was a legal and political sensation. The most serious charge was that Keppel had 'led the whole fleet away' from the French, in a manner that was 'disgraceful to the British flag', but, as it happened, he was acquitted on all charges, amid widespread rejoicing. After the revelry had died down, the Admiral's friend, the 2nd Marquis of Rockingham, built a large Doric column on the high ground at Scholes Coppice, about a mile from his mansion of Wentworth Woodhouse.

To understand the importance of the trial, and what was at stake, we should recall another such event in 1757, when Admiral John Byng had been court-martialled for failing to relieve a British garrison in Minorca. He had been found guilty and executed by firing squad in Portsmouth, an event that was made world famous by Voltaire. In his novel *Candide*, the hero witnesses a similar execution and is told by a phlegmatic Englishman that 'in Britain, we think it is a good idea to put an admiral to death from time to time, to encourage the others' *(pour encourager les autres)*. In real life, Admiral Keppel had participated in Byng's trial but disapproved of the severity of the sentence, and petitioned the Crown for mercy. The result was merely that Byng's execution was postponed for two weeks.

### The Battle of Ushant, 1778
The background to the Battle of Ushant was the American War of Independence. The British had been used to ruling the waves – the lyrics of *Rule, Britannia!* were set to music in 1740 – but then, shortly after the Declaration of Independence in 1776, the Americans had negotiated an alliance with France, and the French Navy was enlisted in their service. The consequence was that, for a time, Britain was unable to resupply her armies in America, and two British armies were forced to surrender at Saratoga (in 1777) and Yorktown (in 1781). By the Treaty of Paris of 1783, George III had to recognise the independence of the Thirteen Colonies, which later became the USA.

Meanwhile, in June 1778, Admiral Keppel took command of HMS *Victory*, with 100 guns and some 900 men on board. This was the same warship whose place in history was secured when she served as Nelson's flagship at Trafalgar in 1805. However, on this occasion, the Admiral led a small squadron in search of the French fleet and encountered an enemy squadron, including the *La Belle Poule* in the Channel, and a far less glorious result than Trafalgar ensued. The British captured the smaller French ships, but two frigates, including *La Belle Poule*, escaped, although thirty had been killed and seventy-two wounded.

The British thought this skirmish inconclusive, but the French classed it as a victory. By way of celebration, the ladies at Versailles invented a new hairstyle called *Belle Poule*, which featured a model ship on top of the head. For his part, Keppel returned to port, having learned from prisoners he had taken that he had been misled by the Admiralty as to the total strength of the French fleet. Instead of seventeen ships of the line at Brest there were thirty-two, but this did not prevent him from being attacked in Parliament for returning from France too soon. Some even compared his conduct with that of Admiral Byng, which naturally led to speculation as to whether Keppel might suffer the same fate.

**A depiction of the Battle of Ushant in 1778, by Théodore Gudin *c.* 1848.**

Keppel put to sea again on 9 July 1778, this time with thirty ships of the line, and encountered a fleet of around the same size near the island of Ushant, off the west coast of Brittany, on the 26th and 27th of that month. Once more, the battle was thought to be inconclusive in Britain, but it was certainly bloody. Each fleet had over 20,000 men, and, according to the evidence given at Keppel's trial, British casualties numbered 133 killed and 373 wounded. Once again, some of the French reached a different conclusion. A 'Prince of the Blood' who took part in the battle was given permission to carry news of it to Paris and Versailles, and he announced a French victory. He even received a standing ovation, and an effigy of Keppel was burnt in the gardens of his family residence. Later reports suggested a different outcome and the prince in question was (like Keppel) accused of misconduct.[1]

Keppel's court martial came about in this way: While the fleet was still at sea, a Whig paper published an article that blamed Sir Hugh Palliser for the inconclusive outcome of the Battle of Ushant. Palliser had commanded HMS *Formidable* there, and had been one of Keppel's vice-admirals, in charge of the Blue Squadron of ten ships.

The Whigs claimed that at a critical moment on the second day of the battle, Palliser had ignored Keppel's signal to bring the Blue Squadron into line and attack the French, and that this had allowed them to escape. Palliser was incensed by this suggestion and demanded that as soon as they returned to port, Keppel should sign a statement to confirm that he had acted properly. Keppel refused to sign, issued an official protest and inserted an account in the *Morning Post* that was very different from Palliser's. There were several further angry exchanges, including a debate in the House of Commons, where both men were MPs, but neither side was willing to back down. Eventually, Palliser brought a capital charge against Keppel to clear his own name. Horace Walpole considered that Palliser acted rashly in doing this, and even said he had evoked 'the astonishment of mankind'.

## The trial of Admiral Keppel

Keppel's trial attracted a great deal of public attention and was particularly acrimonious.[2] While it was taking place, Keppel's and Palliser's ships were both anchored in Portsmouth Harbour, but they had to be kept well apart to prevent fighting between rival crews. However, Keppel's aristocratic supporters rallied to his side. The Dukes of Cumberland, Gloucester, Portland, Richmond and Bolton, and the politicians Edmund Burke and Charles James Fox, all gathered in Portsmouth, while the leader of the Whig party, the 2nd Marquis of Rockingham, took a house there, in which Keppel lived throughout the proceedings.[3]

The atmosphere on board the *Britannia* must have been tense, especially since the prosecutor (Palliser) and the accused (Keppel) both seem to have conducted their own case, though both had legal assistance. There were more than fifty witnesses, consisting of the captains and officers of the British vessels involved in the action, and the evidence, much of it dealing with tedious detail about the sending and receiving of signals, occupies over 300 pages in the report of the trial published soon after its conclusion.[4] There were several sharp exchanges between the two sides and between one of the judges (Admiral Montague) and the witnesses over matters of law and procedure. For reasons we shall see, some observers even thought that Montague and other members of the court were biased in favour of Keppel because of his political views. Keppel objected to Palliser's attempt to make a speech after, as well as before, he had produced his witnesses, and there were clashes between Judge Montague and Captains Beazely of the *Formidable*, Goodhall of the *Defiance*, and Lord Mulgrave of the *Courageux*. Montague asked each of these witnesses, as seamen, what they thought of Keppel's conduct during the battle. Had they seen Keppel do or fail to do anything that would amount to negligence? In each case, the witness was reluctant to answer the question, saying that he was there as a witness of fact and not there to voice an opinion. One might have thought that all three were right about this, but Montague persisted with his line of questioning, and in each case the witness then refused to answer.

In the case of Lord Mulgrave (who was an MP and had become a member of Lord North's Tory government in 1775), Montague asked, 'From your own knowledge and observation, did Admiral Keppel negligently perform his duty on 27 or 28 July?'

Mulgrave replied, 'The term negligence implies a crime. 'Tis for the court to decide, and not me. I have answered to facts.' He went on to say that, if pressed, he would ask the whole court to retire, to form an opinion as to whether it was a proper question, and then give a ruling on the point. At which point, Montague exploded: 'The language you have used, when it goes abroad, will appear strange without doors.' Mulgrave stuck to his guns. One of the other judges agreed with Montague and said, 'I totally disapprove and condemn [Mulgrave's] language.' Nevertheless, the judges did withdraw and, after an adjournment of almost an hour, they delivered their opinion via the Judge Advocate. The ruling was that the witness had 'made use of language unbecoming the dignity of this court' and that the witness must answer the question, whereupon Mulgrave said that he had not intended to give offence, but still declined to answer it.

So far as we know, there were no adverse consequences for these witnesses, but in his opening speech, Keppel referred to their obstinacy and made it clear that in his view the opinions of those present were relevant ('plain speaking, and a full declaration, are the best evidences in a good cause'), although on the other hand, he questioned whether the captain of any single ship could really tell what was going on during a battle. In his view, it was only the Admiral who could see the whole picture.

The other remarkable feature of the trial was the allegation made by Keppel that some of the prosecution's documentary evidence had been tampered with. Thus, he suggested to Captain Hood of the *Robust* that his ship's log had been altered; when Hood claimed that he had 'revised' it for his (Hood's) own protection, he rejected that explanation. Keppel also suggested to Captain Beazley that three highly relevant leaves of the log of the *Formidable* had been removed, and – when this was admitted – Beazley said, 'I do not know, so help me God.' In his closing speech Keppel argued that the evidence had clearly been tampered with 'to exculpate the Prosecutor' (Palliser).

At the end of the proceedings, the court not only dismissed all charges of Misconduct and Neglect of Duty, but found that they were 'MALICIOUS and ILL-FOUNDED, it having appeared that the Admiral, so far from having by misconduct and neglect of duty on the days alluded to, lost an opportunity of rendering essential service to the state, and thereby tarnished the honour of the British Navy, behaved as became a JUDICIOUS, BRAVE and EXPERIENCED OFFICER'.

This verdict was very damning for the prosecution. It meant not only that Keppel should never have been charged, because there was insufficient evidence of his guilt, but also that the prosecutor had an ulterior motive, which could only have been to exculpate himself. Many people must therefore have concluded that Palliser's refusal or inability to follow Keppel's orders had brought disgrace upon the Royal Navy, and after the acquittal, Palliser was forced to go into hiding for fear of his life, while the Whig opposition in Parliament demanded that he be dismissed from all his offices. Indeed, the Earl of Sandwich, who was the first Lord of the Admiralty (and, yes, he did invent the sandwich), came to the same conclusion, and the King wrote to the Prime Minister to say that it was inevitable. Though bitterly resentful, Palliser resigned from the government and even vacated his seat in the Commons ... but this was not the end of the matter.

## Politics in the 1770s

Ostensibly, Keppel and Palliser had much in common. They had both enjoyed distinguished careers in the Royal Navy. Keppel had joined up at the age of 10, sailed round the world with Anson at the age of 15, been promoted post-captain at the age of 19, and seen constant service during the Wars of the Austrian Succession (1740–48) and the Seven Years' War (1756–63). Likewise, Palliser went to sea at the age of 11, was appointed captain at the age of 23, and was instrumental in promoting scientific and exploratory schemes and an early patron of Captain Cook.[5] But the two men could not have been more different when it came to politics. Keppel sat as an MP from 1755 to 1782, Palliser from 1774 to 1784, but whereas Keppel was a Whig, Palliser was a Tory.[6] Throughout the 1770s, Lord North was Prime Minister and the Whigs, led by the 2nd Marquis of Rockingham, were in opposition. On the other hand, Palliser was a government man, who served as Lord of the Admiralty from 1775 to 1779. He had therefore played an important part in organising the Royal Navy for the American war, and in this capacity he had assured the House of Commons that the Navy was in 'a most flourishing state' and that 'the whole fleet would be completely manned in a very short time'. As we have seen, this proved to be very far from the truth. When Keppel first arrived in Portsmouth in March 1778, he found only six ships that were seaworthy, whereas Palliser had led him to believe that twenty would be immediately available. Moreover, like many Whigs, Keppel had been reluctant to serve in the war against the colonists in the first place.

Keppel's trial was consequently a highly political event and was extensively reported in newspapers and in the *Gentleman's Magazine*. Further, his acquittal was an important victory, not only for Keppel, but for the Rockingham Whigs. The Cambridge historian Herbert Butterfield summed the position up over half a century ago:

> In the period of peace the British had neglected their navy, and in the last four or five years they had failed duly to appreciate the considerable revival that had been taking place in the maritime power of France. In 1778 Admiral Keppel had found the fleet insufficient for coping with a single Bourbon power; and the fiasco in the Channel during the first year's campaign against France had led to a renewal of faction in the navy, a foolish trial of Keppel by court martial, and a bitter parliamentary attack upon [Sir Hugh Palliser] in the early months of 1779. Henceforward Sandwich was never allowed to forget how he had once declared that head of the Admiralty to be worthy of execution who should fail to maintain a navy capable of meeting the combined forces of France and Spain.[7]

Keppel's acquittal was greeted by the Whigs with widespread rejoicing. Portsmouth was illuminated, and the ships of the East India Company fired a nineteen-gun salute. Keppel was carried through the streets to the strains of 'See the conquering hero comes', before retiring to his house to celebrate with over sixty captains. In London, both Houses of Parliament gave him a vote of thanks, and he was granted the Freedom of the City. The London mob celebrated by breaking the Prime Minister's windows, smashing up

Palliser's house in Pall Mall and burning his effigy on Tower Hill. In the city of York, Palliser's sister's home was demolished, while all over the country, landlords changed the name of their pub to The Keppel's Head.

## The trial of Sir Hugh Palliser

One might have thought that the show was over in Portsmouth, but this was not so. Following Keppel's acquittal, the Lords of the Admiralty ordered an inquiry, because in their view there were 'several circumstances in the minutes of the trial of an incriminating nature against Vice-Admiral Sir Hugh Palliser'. As result, he was now court-martialled, again in Portsmouth Harbour, but this time on board HMS *Sandwich*.[8] The court sat from 12 April to 5 May 1779, and again, no stone was left unturned. Keppel and numerous witnesses gave evidence and were cross-examined by Palliser, who presented his defence in person. There were several arguments about the law (including one concerning the reliability of log books, when they had been written up at sea, in the middle of a battle). Palliser objected to the broad and vague nature of the charges against him, protesting that this made it difficult for him to defend himself. However, his major objection was that the proceedings were motivated by party political prejudice and personal animosity: Keppel was a snake in the grass, who had repeatedly assured him that he (Palliser) had done all that a conscientious officer could do on the day of the battle, but was now trying to condemn him to the same fate as the unfortunate Admiral Byng.

There was a dispute concerning the reliability of some of the testimony given by Captain Harland of HMS *Queen*. Harland attempted to refer to newspaper reports, though he admitted that they were sometimes 'stupidly or artfully mangled'. The Judge Advocate gave him a severe dressing-down, saying that the court would 'have nothing to do with [such reports]', that they were 'foreign to the question and the business of the trial', and could not be 'admitted to stand part of the minutes'. This objection to evidence that was at the least hearsay would seem to be obvious, but Harland argued that the court ought to listen to all his evidence and judge for itself what it was worth, rather than refuse to listen to it at all. He added that this had been the practice in every other court martial he had ever attended, but the court did not agree.

The nub of the prosecution this time was that Keppel had sent a signal to Palliser, at about 5.00 pm on 28 July, ordering him to get into line and attack the French (described by Palliser as 'the old and insidious enemy'). Indeed, Keppel testified that he had waited for several hours, with mounting impatience and anxiety, for Palliser to obey, but had seen no evidence that he would; Palliser replied that he had never received any such signal. Furthermore, even if he had, he could not possibly have done as his admiral wished, because his ship was 'a perfect wreck' after doing the bulk of the fighting thus far. Lastly, he had thought at the time that Keppel was most unlikely to resume any attack on the French before the following morning.

The verdict once again exonerated the prisoner from any misconduct or neglect of duty. Indeed, the court found that Palliser's behaviour was 'in many respects highly exemplary and meritorious'. However, the court did think that Palliser deserved censure for his failure to inform Keppel that the *Formidable* was so badly disabled, and the acquittal did not lead to any wider exoneration. Palliser immediately applied to be restored to his lieutenant generalship of marines, without success, and the Whigs resumed their attacks on him in Parliament and in the press. Early in 1780, Sandwich succeeded in obtaining for Palliser the appointment as governor of Greenwich Hospital. Although he did not stand again as MP for Scarborough at the general election, he was returned unopposed for Huntingdon, in the government's interest. Nevertheless, when he re-entered the Commons, he was immediately attacked again by the opposition. In his own words, he now felt that he was 'the most injured character in the kingdom'.

### Keppel's Column

Keppel's acquittal continued to be celebrated. In 1773, the 2nd Marquis of Rockingham had asked John Carr of York, his architect, to design a landscape feature that 'would please the eye' on the southern boundary of Wentworth Park. Carr designed a 40-foot tower to be surmounted by an obelisk – one of the four that had once stood in the garden to the west of the mansion. John Hobson, the estate mason, made an estimate of £115-3s-0d for the work. Progress was slow and in 1776 the Marquis asked for a revised estimate for raising the column by a further 78 feet. In 1779, the Marquis changed his mind again and decided to honour his friend and political ally Admiral Keppel to celebrate his acquittal. He now proposed that the column should be 150 feet high with a statue of Keppel, 30 feet high, on the top and four ships' prows pointing out of its base. The design was impractical, but the Marquis was keen for the work to be completed, so they settled on a column of 115 feet.[9]

The first visit to the column took place in October 1780, when several newspapers in different parts of the country reported a gathering of Rockingham, his friends, and local dignitaries, though, apparently, not the eponymous Admiral:

> We hear from Yorkshire, that on the first inst. was finished at Scholes Coppice, near Wentworth House, an elegant column, built by the Marquis of Rockingham, in honour of the acquittal of Admiral Keppel. It is 120 feet in height, and ascended by 220 steps. On the Monday following, a number of the nobility and gentry assembled on the top to drink the health of the Admiral, amongst whom were the noble Marquis, the Earl of Effingham, Lord G.A. Cavendish, Hon Mr. Fitzwilliam, Mr. Weddell, Mr Barwell, Mr. Buck, etc., etc. As soon as they appeared in the wood, they were saluted by three cheers, accompanied by the discharges of 21 pieces of cannon; French horns, etc. An elegant cold collation was provided, with a great plenty of wines, etc. Several hogsheads of ale were given to the populace. The Union flag was displayed on top of the column, with the words 'Admiral Keppel forever, the pride and glory of Great Britain'.

The 2nd Marquis of Rockingham died at the age of 52, two years after he had stood on top of Keppel's Column on the inaugural visit. He was buried in York Minster, but is commemorated in his monument at the bottom of Wentworth Park, along with eight of the Whigs, including Augustus Keppel and the firebrand Charles James Fox.

Keppel's Column took its place alongside several other monuments in and around Wentworth Park. It was mentioned by the local poet Ebenezer Elliott (1781–1849), known as 'the Corn Law Rhymer', in *The Ranter*:

> Up, sluggards, up!
> Up, climb the oak-crown'd summit. Hoober Stand,
> And Keppel's Pillar, gaze on Wentworth's Halls,
> And misty lakes, that brighten and expand,
> And distant hills, that watch the western strand.

The child who wrote to 'Captain Trim' of the *Sheffield Weekly Telegraph*, published on Saturday, 28 May 1904, told the readers that he, his father and brother and two playmates had taken a walk up Wentworth Park during the Whit holidays that year and

**A group of visitors at the top of Keppel's Column,** *c.* **1910.** *William Herbert Barraclough*

had 'ascended the column and had a look round'. The column came to be regarded as a 'romantic spot' and, according to 'Countryman' (writing in the *Leeds Mercury* for 23 August 1939), it was one from which one could enjoy a truly spectacular view, interrupted by the sight of only one pithead, in the days when coal mining had transformed the appearance of many local beauty spots. We may wonder, however, if we can trust this 'Countryman', since he counted only 155 steps. There are in fact 217.[10]

Older people can still remember that the column was once called 'Scholes Coppy', after the coppice wood nearby, and some even remember paying a small amount before ascending the staircase inside to emerge on the top. Numerous family photographs and postcards survive that show the column from the late Victorian period onwards. It is clear that it was a popular attraction. At Easter and on Sundays in summer, locals would visit and picnic nearby. One family who lived in a neighbouring cottage used an old tramcar to serve teas, ice cream and sweets. Children could have donkey rides. From the 1940s until 1960, the charge for climbing to the top was 2d for adults and 1d for children, payable to Cyril White, woodman on the Fitzwilliam estate who lived in the lodge at Scholes. Some local doctors even suggested that patients with chest complaints should climb the steps to the top and breathe deeply!

Keppel's Column still stands, though it was closed to the public in 1962. It can, however, be viewed close up, by means of videos taken by drone and posted on the internet. These show that the exterior of the structure is intact, though the railings around the top are incomplete, and they allow the virtual visitor to enjoy splendid views all around. In early 2020, it was announced that money had been secured for structural repairs. Perhaps one day it will again be possible to climb the steps and take in the view from the top.

**Visitors posing at the base of the Column.** *William Herbert Barraclough*

*Chapter 6*

# THE PARK, GARDENS AND MENAGERIE AT WENTWORTH WOODHOUSE

When the name Wentworth Woodhouse is mentioned most readers will think only of the house, but the house is surrounded by an extensive park and gardens and once contained a menagerie full of exotic birds and animals. And just as in the past, when it was owned by the Wentworth and Fitzwilliam families, visitors can still go on garden tours or walk through the park on public footpaths and visit those parts of the garden that are now incorporated into Wentworth Garden Centre.

## The park

At its greatest extent, the park was 9 miles in circumference, largely walled, with park lodges, which still exist, around its perimeter, one of them on Hague Lane in the style of a Greek temple. One famous writer, the agriculturist Arthur Young, said in 1768 that the park 'is one of the most exquisite spots in the world'. And as it has been for centuries, the park is still the home to a herd of red deer, which can be seen grazing among the trees. And yet on the earliest known maps of South Yorkshire, John Speed's map of Yorkshire of 1610 and Joan Blaeu's map *c*. 1648, *Ducatus Eboracensis Anglice Yorkshire*, the park is not shown, although the neighbouring parks at Stainborough and Tankersley are. The first detailed map of the park is on John Warburton's map of Yorkshire of 1720. But this is inaccurate in that it has the mount (see below), which was in the gardens, in the centre of the park, and has the mansion on the south-east corner of the park instead of to the west. An interesting engraving survives from 1728 showing a deer shed, deer and some of the park wall.[1] Warburton's map does however show the stream in whose valley the lakes were later constructed, flowing eastwards to the south of the park past Morley and through Greasbrough towards the river Don. The early engraving shows numerous fish ponds (the 1st Marquis being an enthusiastic breeder of goldfish, tench and carp) and Morley Pond. In 1737, the Marquis wrote, 'a piece of water of three acres was made for a Serpentine river'.[2]

For centuries the park has been studded with grand trees, both native and introduced, and with natural and planted woodland. The woods include Trowles Wood, Shire Oaks Wood, Mausoleum Wood, Cortworth Wood, Temple Hill Plantation and Rockingham

**The Doric Lodge on Hague Lane, built in the style of a Greek temple.**

Wood. The most interesting of these in terms of origin and early use is Rockingham Wood, or as it was earlier called, Lady Rockingham's Wood. This wood is a plantation on the former Greasbrough Common, which was incorporated into the park after the enclosure of the common in 1728, of which 261 acres came into the possession of the future 1st Marquis, who incorporated it into the park. The wood was protected from grazing deer by a deep ditch along parts of the southern and northern edges and along the whole of the western boundary, in the last case backed by a revetted stone wall. Jefferys' map of 1771 shows paths round the wood just inside its perimeter. Why it is called Lady's Rockingham's Wood is not clear: it may have been planted at her suggestion; she may also have been involved in its planting and layout. She was obviously a frequent visitor to the wood, as reflected in the record left by Richard Pococke in August 1750:

> I went with them [the Marquis & Lady Rockingham] to my Lady's wood, where there is a little house in which a batchelor may live, offices

underground. We walked round the wood, drank tea, and returned, and my lady engaged me to dine that day in the wood.[3]

Rockingham Wood was also visited by Arthur Young during his northern tour in 1768–70, and he described it in some detail:

> The wood is cut into winding walks of which there is a great variety; in part of it, on a small hill of shaven grass, is a house for repasts in hot weather. The dining room is 32 feet by 16 feet, very neatly fitted up; the chimney-pieces of white marble of a judicious simplicity, the bow-windows remarkably light and airy. Adjoining is a little drawing-room hung with Indian paper, and a large closet and with book cases; beneath are a kitchen and other offices.[4]

When one of the authors was undertaking a research report on Rotherham's ancient woods on behalf of Rotherham Metropolitan Borough Council and English Nature in 1991, Rockingham Wood was a commercial wood used for rearing pheasants.

**The magnificent stable block designed by John Carr and built from 1768 to 1789.**

It contained a gamekeeper's cottage and its most memorable features were the rows of hanging shot predators: crows, rooks and mostly magpies.

A beautiful feature of the park is the string of lakes – Morley Pond, Dog Kennel Pond and Mill Dam, which make a Serpentine Lake wriggling through the landscape. Morley Pond was shown on the engraving of 1728 and Scholes, Morley and Dog Kennel ponds are all shown on Jefferys' map of 1771 and a survey of 1783. They were the subject of design improvements by the famous landscape gardener Humphry Repton, in about 1790, and were expanded in the nineteenth century. It was Repton who suggested building the bridge between Morley Pond and Dog Kennel Pond to give the impression of a flowing river rather than separate lakes. Local people from Greasbrough used to go skating on the lakes in harsh winters, with blazing torches illuminating the scene at night. The lakes are now used by anglers.

For hundreds of years, the park has also been adorned with magnificent monuments: a Doric temple, the Mausoleum and Keppel's Column (which is now located outside the park). The Doric temple, which dates from the 1740s, is attributed to the 1st Marquis's architect Henry Flitcroft. It is octagonal in shape with a vaulted dome, and offers views over the park and to the countryside to the south and south-west. It stands on the upper slope of a large hill. The 2nd Marquis engaged

estate workmen to remove part of the hill but after years of quarrying, Humphry Repton, in 1790, suggested to the 4th Earl Fitzwilliam that tree planting would make a better rural scene, and it has been an eye-catcher near the summit of the wooded hill ever since.[5]

The Mausoleum is not a mausoleum in the real sense because the 2nd Marquis, who was a leading Whig politician and was Prime Minister twice, is buried in York Minster. It is a cenotaph, i.e. a monument to his memory. It was built on behalf of the 2nd Marquis's nephew, the 4th Earl Fitzwilliam, who inherited the Wentworth estates in 1782. It was designed by John Carr over a four-year period from 1784 to 1788. Outside stand the obelisks that once decorated the gardens to the west of the Baroque mansion. The ground floor of the Mausoleum is an enclosed hall containing a life-size marble statue of the robed Marquis. Around the walls are niches containing busts of eight of his close political allies: Charles James Fox, Edmund Burke, Lord John Cavendish, John Lee, the Duke of Portland, Frederick Montague, Sir George Savile and Admiral Augustus Keppel. The original marble busts have been replaced by plaster casts. Because of the presence of the Mausoleum and Keppel's Column, the Doric temple in the park and the Ionic temple in the garden (see below), as well as the Palladian mansion (Palladianism had become the 'national style'), some writers have dubbed the landscape at Wentworth a 'political landscape' or an 'Orthodox Whig Landscape'.[6]

And the stable block must not be forgotten. One eighteenth-century visitor said the stable block was more like a palace than a home for horses. Even today, some first-time visitors entering the park think it is the mansion. It was designed by John Carr, the York architect, and built from 1768 to 1789. It was built around a square courtyard with a riding school at the southern end. There is a large fountain in the courtyard. It originally housed carriage and riding horses, as well as carriages and coaches, and later, motor cars. In the 1891census, thirty stable employees were recorded living in the stables, and staff still lived in the stable block until the end of the 1940s. In the period from 1950 to 1986, when Lady Mabel College and Sheffield City Polytechnic occupied Wentworth Woodhouse, the stable block was converted into office and teaching accommodation.

### The formal ornamental gardens in 1728

The first detailed record of the ornamental gardens at Wentworth Woodhouse is visual. It is in the form of an engraving of 1728 showing the ornamental gardens stretching from the westward-facing Baroque front of the mansion all the way to Hague Lane.[7] And these early ornamental gardens retain features characteristic of formal gardens that were laid out in the Tudor and Stuart period. Immediately in front of the Baroque mansion was a large lawn divided into four by a wide path running north to south and a central drive leading westwards towards Hague Lane. In the centre of each quarter of the lawn stood a large obelisk. The future 1st Marquis said that the obelisks were in position in 1729, although he may have regretted their positioning when Horace Walpole said the view looked like a bowling alley! On the south side of the lawn were five rows of what appear to be pleached trees, probably fruit trees, and beyond these, near the south wall, other planted trees, and placed

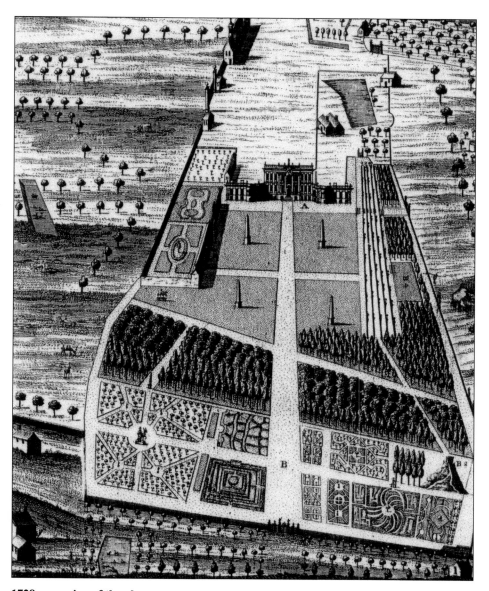

**1728 engraving of the pleasure grounds stretching westwards from the Baroque mansion.**
*Bodleian Library, University of Oxford, Gough Maps 35, Folio 48*

amongst them what was probably a bowling green. On the north side of the lawn were three walled beds. West of the lawn was another area of planted trees and beyond this a large area laid out mostly as knot gardens, one in a complicated whorl pattern and another looking like a maze. There were two statues on the walks between the beds. At the southern end of this part of the garden was a mount with winding paths leading to the summit, where there was a tower.

## Informalisation of the gardens

When the kitchen gardens (see below) were moved from the east of the house to the west and the Palladian front became the 'show off' part of the house, the formal gardens to the west were either obliterated or changed in character. The obelisks in front of the Baroque mansion were moved and eventually placed around the Mausoleum. Although the main central drive towards Hague Lane remained – against the advice of Humphry Repton, who suggested much more winding pathways – a large part of the gardens from the early nineteenth century took on a much more informal character, with many planted trees, native and exotic, together with beds of perennial and annual flowers. Writing in 1888, the correspondent from the *Illustrated London News*, in a long, copiously illustrated piece about Wentworth Woodhouse at the time of the 6th Earl's and Countess's golden wedding, said that the Baroque mansion 'overlooks a lovely greensward bordered with rare trees of the softest, deep colour'. He went on to say that 'these gardens are the prettiest of the old fashion that I have ever seen', noting that 'one most lovely bed of violas of a glowing purple-blue is quite unforgettable'.[8] It was this part of the gardens that was cruelly dug up at the behest of Emmanuel Shinwell, Minister of Fuel and Power, in his pursuit of opencast coal.[9] Roger Dataller, local writer and broadcaster, wrote a scathing article in the *Northern Review* in September 1946 about the 'frontal attack upon the gardens at Wentworth Woodhouse', which he called 'a piece of vandalism'. He said he had visited the site 'just before the final onset' and that he had seen 'great tracks scored in the ground, daffodil bulbs uprooted by the thousand, and white and wounded trees tumbled in the grasses'. Since then, this part of

**Camellia House, awaiting restoration.**

the gardens has been renovated and replanted in a patchwork informal style, and garden tours are now in operation, including a February snowdrop walk.

The main central drive was once surfaced with red ash and this was the scene of a very special job while the family lived at the house. Every Saturday morning, one of the gardeners, armed with a special brush about a metre wide in a wooden frame with long bristles and two handles, smoothed the drive all the way from the main door of the Baroque front to the door in the wall of the kitchen garden that led to Hague Lane. Altogether it is said that he would make up to eight or ten trips back and forth along the drive. All this was because on fine summer Sundays the family and their guests would walk along the drive to the service in the parish church.

The gardens contain three important buildings: the Ionic Temple, which betrays the influence of continental classical architecture; the Camellia House, which was for show and relaxation; and the Ice House, which had a utilitarian purpose. The Ionic Temple, dating from *c.* 1735, which stands at the western end of the terrace wall that bounds the gardens to the north, has been attributed to the 1st Marquis's architect, Henry Flitcroft. Inside is a marble sculpture of Hercules slaying a mythical beast. Documents from 1812–22 reveal that a new glasshouse, the Camellia House, was being built on the site of the old garden greenhouse. The documents record the digging of foundations, masons' and carpenters' work, and the use of flags, glass and slate in its construction.

How did the aristocrats of the eighteenth and nineteenth centuries keep their wine cool and their meat and fish fresh? What must be remembered is that domestic refrigerators were not invented until the late nineteenth century. So they had icehouses in which they kept crushed ice, which supplied them for most of the year. The ice was obtained from the lakes and ponds in their parks and gardens in deepest winter. It was the head gardener's responsibility to collect and store the ice. Teams of men with picks and shovels would break up the ice on the ponds and lakes, take it by horse and cart across the park to an icehouse near the mansion. Icehouses usually had an ornamental entrance, beyond which there was a passage, often with two or three internal doors at intervals to increase insulation. At the end of the passage there would be a domed storage chamber, which was sunk below ground level and in which the crushed ice was placed. The one at Wentworth Woodhouse was built in 1735 and originally had a thatched roof. It still survives, located to the east of the stable block.

## The Japanese and Italian gardens

These two gardens now lie within the bounds of Wentworth Garden Centre, to the south of the slip garden. The two gardens are entered through an arched gateway. A gate once existed that bore the invitation 'Come into the garden Maud', placed there by the 7th Earl Fitzwilliam for his countess, who was an enthusiastic gardener. A path leads to a sunken Japanese garden, which is said to have been designed by Maud. There was a much publicised and widely reported Japan-British exhibition at the White City in London in 1910, which contained two large Japanese gardens. The gardens and their plants were enthusiastically written about in the gardening journals of the day and following the exhibition a number of well-known gardens were created in the Japanese style. Perhaps Countess Maud visited the exhibition or some of the newly created gardens and came back to Wentworth to instil a Japanese element there. The site seems to have been adapted from a pre-existing fern and rock garden. Although neglected for more than fifty years, a number of characteristic features of Japanese gardens still survive, including the pond against the quarry wall, a cascade (now dry), the remains of a number of Japanese lanterns and Japanese plants, including maples and cherries. In the past there was a set of stepping stones across the pond and a bridge high over it. A peculiar feature beside the pond comprises open doorways (the remains of the hinges that held the missing doors can still be seen) of a series of duck houses where waterfowl from the pond could find security. Just outside the Japanese garden on the edge of the Italian garden is Countess Maud's teahouse, not in the Japanese style but covered by an ancient wisteria, which is native to Japan.

To the north of the sunken Japanese garden is a more formal garden, sometimes known as the Italian garden. Water features form an important part of the garden here. There is a small pond filled with irises and two straight-edged canals, the longer of the two, running parallel to the slip garden wall, being crossed by two zigzag bridges. There are some interesting trees in this part of the garden, including two weeping copper beeches. Stone steps lead up a steep grassy bank at the western end of the canal to another sunken garden edged with three broad planted terraces that surround a rectangular pool with a fountain. Beyond this sunken garden, leading to a view over the top of the quarry to the pond in the Japanese garden below, are a series of grassed areas bounded by cut yew hedges.

**The kitchen garden**

A kitchen garden is shown on Fairbank's map of 1778, to the east of the mansion. Here the 1st Marquis grew pineapples, as described in Chapter 3. These were prized fruits, not necessarily to be eaten, but to be gazed at with envy. He also cultivated grapes. In 1746, he presented to King George II, 'one bunch of Frontiniak Grapes & one of Muscardine perfectly ripe' to mark the victory over the Jacobites.[10] In 1750, Richard Pococke described the splendid watermelons and 'moseh' (bananas) being grown at Wentworth. These kitchen gardens were replaced in the 1780s by a new kitchen garden to the west, which involved the rerouting of Hague Lane westwards to accommodate it. This new area contained a walled kitchen garden created largely under the supervision of John Carr of York. Rectangular in shape, it covered 4 acres and was surrounded by 12-foot high brick walls. These survive and form the nucleus of Wentworth Garden Centre. The north and south walls of the kitchen garden were hot walls, that is, they had internal flues fuelled by furnaces with the hot air escaping through chimneys in the tops of the walls. The internal layout of the walled kitchen garden was a typical cross-shaped arrangement of four sections, separated and surrounded by broad paths. The east-west path formed part of a longer pathway that in one direction went through the garden gate (the gate posts being surmounted by statues of Lucretia and Collatinus) to the mansion, and in the other through a door in the west wall onto Hague Lane and across to Church Drive to Wentworth church. To the north of the walled garden a new orchard was set out, and to the north-east was a large pond shared by the gardens and the adjacent Home Farm. To the south of the walled garden, lying between the shelter of the south wall and

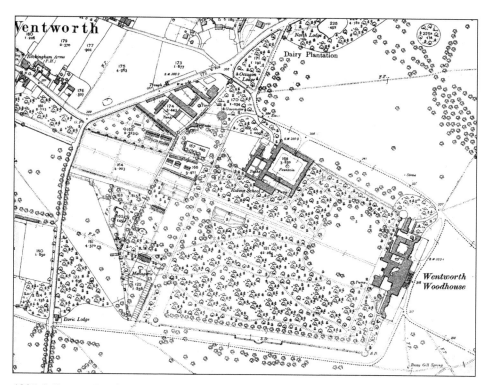

**1905 O.S. map showing the rectangular kitchen garden, Home Farm, stable block and gardens to the west of the mansion.**

a sunken fence, was a so-called 'slip garden', which provided further sheltered space for fruit trees and beds of vegetables.

Orders were placed far and wide with seedsmen and nurserymen to supply plants and seeds for the kitchen garden – G.&J. Telford of York and J.G. Perfect of Pontefract cropping up most commonly in the order books in the eighteenth century, and Perfects and Backhouse of York in the nineteenth century. The variety of vegetables purchased was enormous. For example, the orders from Telford's and Perfects in 1790 consisted of seven varieties of beans, six varieties of peas, six varieties of lettuce, four varieties of cabbage and three of broccoli. They also bought celery, parsnip, spinach, red beet, endive, asparagus and two varieties each of onion, turnip and radish. Also included were now rarely heard-of vegetables: orache, cardoon, salsify and scorzonera. Orders were also placed for the fruits growing up the kitchen garden walls and under glass – peaches, nectarines, apricots, oranges and grapes – and in the orchard to the north of the kitchen garden – apples, pears, cherries and hazels (for their nuts).[11]

A list of gardeners in August 1794 names twenty-seven individuals, with Benjamin Henderson, the head gardener, and four female gardeners. In the 1850s, there were forty to fifty gardeners at Wentworth.

### Garden glasshouses and vineries

In 1908, the Edinburgh firm of Mackenzie & Moncur built a large plant house and new vineries for the 7th Earl Fitzwilliam just to the east of the walled kitchen garden. This magnificent glasshouse comprised a central palm and plant corridor 200 feet long and 20 feet wide, with seven subsidiary houses, each 35 feet long, on the south side and seven on the north side, each 40 feet long. All the subsidiary houses were span shape, with cast iron moulded gutters.

The plant house was open to the public on special occasions every year and a cine film survives, made by local dentist Willie Thorne, which shows it in its pomp.[12] At that time the central corridor and show house were full of flowering plants, including hibiscus, bird of paradise, abutilons, daturas, arum lilies, calceolarias, hydrangeas, amaryllis, begonias, fuchsias, camellias and chrysanthemums. The orchid house was in full bloom and the fernery in rampant growth. There were also magnificent banana plants carrying large bunches of fruit. Sadly, the entire plant house was demolished in the 1950s.

The vineries were 88 feet long divided into six houses, each just over 30 feet long and 16 feet wide, with one central passage 6 feet wide. They were built of best Russian redwood, with framing and sills of jarrah wood, in a lean-to shape against a high wall. A range of sheds 18 feet wide and the same length as the vineries was located behind, comprising a boiler house, mushroom house, rhubarb house, potting house, central passage, office, grape room, fruit room and shed. In the grape house were racks for special bottles that held sugar, water and charcoal. The stalk of a bunch of grapes could be inserted into the necks of the bottles to keep them fresh. The cost was £4,558-13s. A further £75 was added for putting in a central tower of the glasshouse. The vinery, like the plant house, has now disappeared, but its high brick-built back wall and the work and storage sheds behind it have survived, although they are inaccessible to the public.

**The central corridor of the 1908 glasshouse.** *Pauline & Michael Bentley*

## The menagerie

By the eighteenth century, scores of aristocrats owned large collections of wild beasts and birds for their amusement and interest, and to adorn their parks and pleasure grounds. There was a menagerie at Wentworth Woodhouse for almost 200 years. It was first mentioned in 1737 by the future 1st Marquis of Rockingham when he noted in his journal that 'the new Menagery [was] taken in'. The following year he wrote, 'the pavilion [a teahouse] and Green House [later the Camellia House] at the upper end of the menagerie were all then Built'.[13] The menagerie is still clearly marked and named on the large scale (25 inches to 1 mile) Ordnance Survey maps published in 1905 and 1930. And this menagerie over the years contained mammals and birds from every corner of the world: North and South America, Africa, Asia and Australasia, besides rare and colourful species from Britain and the rest of Europe. The menagerie stretched away to the south of the Camellia House, including what is now the southern part of the car park at Wentworth Garden Centre.

The menagerie was impressing visitors from an early date. In 1750, Richard Pococke wrote:

> Just by this [Ionic] temple is the menagery in front of the green house, containing a prodigious number of foreign birds, particularly, gold and pencil pheasants, cockatoos, Mallocca doves, etc, etc. The green-house is very spacious, and behind it a neat agreeable room for drinking tea.[14]

When Arthur Young visited in 1768, he said that the aviary was housed in a 'light Chinese building of a very pleasing design stocked with Canary and other foreign birds', which were 'kept alive in winter by means of hot walls at the back of the building; the front being open net-work in compartments'.

From the late eighteenth and throughout the nineteenth century there are detailed records of animals and birds in the menagerie and of their careful management.[15] For example, in June 1788, William Stear was paid for the freight and keep of a moose deer from 'Goul Bridge to Cinder Bridge'. It had obviously been brought from the east coast via Goole on the Humber, on the navigable river Don, and then along the Greasbrough Canal to its terminus at Cinder Bridge, just to the east of Wentworth Park. In November of the same year, Daniel Whealand was paid £7-10s-0d for bringing another moose deer 'from America'. In 1794, John Burgan was paid £8 for his post as pheasant keeper in the menagerie, and in 1808, John Salkeld was paid for his painter's work on the pheasant pens.

The variety of animals and birds in the menagerie in the nineteenth century is astonishing. Altogether, records have been found of eighty-six species: sixty-one species of birds and twenty-five species of mammals (including the buffaloes in the park). The birds included four species of eagle, four species of owl, three species of pheasants, two species of seabirds (cormorant and guillemot), emu, black swan and trumpeter swan. Among interesting yet uncommon European species were shrike, golden oriole and a kingfisher (and its nest!). Mammals included: from South America, alpacas, agoutis (a small forest browser), a tapir and a tiger cat; from Africa, an African goat, mongoose rat and three species of lemur, including the ring-tailed lemur; from Asia, an Indian antelope, an axis deer, a Java hare and a cashmere goat; from Australia, a wombat and female kangaroo (with a joey in its pouch); and from North America, a raccoon and an American brown bear. Are we to assume that the bear was kept in the bear pit, which is located next to the Japanese garden?

There are three remarkable records that tell us about the ardent desire to collect and breed rare animals and the family's attitude to the animals and birds in their care. The first is an entry in the account books for 1841, which records the payment of £31-9s-1d

**The 5th Earl and Countess admiring their newly acquired llamas from Chile.** *Eric Leslie*

for four llamas from Arica in northern Chile and their transport to Liverpool at a cost of £20-15s-0d. The second is that later the same year, on 9 September, the *Doncaster Gazette* reported the 'birth of an extraordinary nature … at the menagerie at Wentworth Woodhouse. The Noble Earl Fitzwilliam is in possession of a male and female llama … very rare in this country … The female has produced one young one perfectly white in colour and healthy in appearance'. The third is a report in the *Sheffield Daily Telegraph* in 1873 about a visit to the menagerie organised for the 6th Earl's coal miners. They were guided around by a 'genial old lady', presumably one of the Earl's menagerie keepers, who pointed out 'the ostrich, the emu, the armadillo, the orang-outang, and the chimpanzee' who 'was fed on port wine and biscuits and attended to just as if he had been a Christian'. That the menagerie keepers at Wentworth Woodhouse were held in high regard is reflected in the fact that James Thompson was recorded as the menagerie keeper in the 1851 census when he was living at Friar House, but by 1861, he was Keeper of Animals in the Zoological Gardens at Regent's Park in London.

Veterinary surgeons made regular visits and the keepers provided the best living conditions for the animals that they could. Accounts show food being purchased – 'sheeps Heads and Hearts for the Eagle', rabbits, mice, seeds, corn and grain. Inevitably some animals died of illness and old age, and a museum was created at the back of what is now the Camellia House for displaying stuffed animals and birds, and mounted skeletons. From the 1830s to the 1850s, Hugh Reid was paid an annual fee for 'preserving and stuffing birds and providing them with cages'. Reid was a taxidermist of some renown who lived in French Gate in Doncaster. In 1841, H. Chapman was paid £4-5s-0d for 'mounting the skeleton of an Antelope' and in 1843, Charles Cooper was paid £12-13s-0d for 'preparing skeletons of llama'.

No evidence has been found of animals being kept in the menagerie during the twentieth century, although an aviary seemed to be in existence until the 1940s. At the time of writing, the Wentworth Woodhouse Preservation Trust has received funding from the Heritage Lottery Fund to draw up detailed plans for the restoration of the Camellia House, the riding school and the southern range of the stables. The hope is to transform the Camellia House into a café and evening events venue whilst retaining the camellias, believed to be the oldest and rarest in the Western world. The park is now maintained by the Wentworth Amenities Trust. The 83 acres of gardens owned by the Wentworth Woodhouse Preservation Trust are cared for by the head gardener and a team of volunteers. Guided walks are held regularly. The Japanese and Italian gardens have been restored by Wentworth Garden Centre and visitors can enjoy the gardens throughout the year for a small entrance fee.

*Chapter 7*

# WENTWORTH, THE FITZWILLIAMS' ESTATE VILLAGE AND ELSECAR, THEIR 'MODEL' INDUSTRIAL VILLAGE

**Wentworth**

Wentworth village is neat and simply laid out and has the character of a village set deep in rural England rather than in a highly urbanised region. The first obvious features of interest to be encountered when approaching the village from the west are the almshouses and former school at Barrow, which date from the early eighteenth century. But these are a mere prelude to the village proper, which starts with the ruined, predominantly medieval church and its surrounding graveyard and then stretches eastwards, largely confined to one street, Main Street, with farmsteads, cottages, public houses and shops, almost all in local stone, including the roof tiles. At the end of the village is the former Home Farm beside the entrance to the park, marked by a park lodge, the Octagon Lodge, and this together with the exclusive use of one colour of paint – Wentworth green – reveal that Wentworth was until quite recently an estate village.

The almshouses and the former Barrow School, as noted above, lie just to the west of the village. Wentworth Barrow School was founded by the Hon. Thomas Watson-Wentworth in 1716, 'for fifty poor children'. It closed in 1943. The complex of buildings originally included a schoolroom, a house for the schoolmaster and a group of almshouses arranged around a quadrangle. It was enlarged in 1892. The big schoolroom contained a three-tier gallery along the south wall, an open fire in the centre of the north wall (with the head teacher's desk close to it), two blackboards and a harmonium. It is said that in the playground the boys played football with anything that would roll, from a potty to a pig's bladder. Behind the old school lie the old almshouses, or hospital, as it was originally called. The hospital was built by Thomas Watson-Wentworth in accordance with his uncle's (the 2nd Earl of Strafford) will. Built of brick with stone slated roofs, around a pleasant grassed courtyard, the former almshouses are still lived in by the retired. There were originally twelve apartments but eight of these have now

**Main Street, Wentworth, in the early twentieth century.** *Chris Sharp*

been converted into four, and the block can accommodate four couples and four single occupants. In the eighteenth century, the occupants (retired estate workers or former tenants) wore a badge on the shoulder of a cape provided by the estate. In 1881, there were thirteen occupants, eleven of them in their seventies and seven of them described as 'paupers'.

On the other side of the road from the almshouses and Barrow School is a less obvious feature. It is a cottage with a window sticking out, through which it is possible to easily see up and down the road. This was originally one of two toll keepers' cottages. In the eighteenth and early nineteenth centuries, almost all of the country's main roads became turnpike roads. Before roads were turnpiked, it was the responsibility of individual parishes and townships to maintain the roads within their boundaries. However, there was such an increase in road traffic in the eighteenth and early nineteenth centuries that local communities could no longer cope. The answer was to form what were called 'turnpike trusts', which covered long, named stretches of highway. The trusts were empowered by Parliament to make the roads toll roads, the tolls being used for road maintenance and, it was hoped, to make a profit for the trusts. The word 'turnpike' refers to an earlier practice of using a bar full of spikes to bar the way. It would be lifted to allow access. The toll cottage at Barrow was on the turnpike road from Rotherham to Barnsley. This road came from Rotherham via Greasbrough and Nether Haugh into

Wentworth village and then continued to the main Sheffield to Wakefield road (the modern A6135), which had been turnpiked in 1758. The turnpike road from Rotherham through Wentworth village was turnpiked in 1764 at the instigation of the 2nd Marquis of Rockingham.

Wentworth School, now Wentworth Primary School, which lies opposite the old church, was opened in 1837 as a mixed infant and girls' school. The 5th Earl Fitzwilliam gave the land and contributed to the building costs. He also established the Wentworth Charity, which provided clothes and a free education for twenty-five boys and twenty-five girls. In 1841, a report stated that 'this is a real school ... they are instructed, not merely dragged along in the ruts of the old road'.

The remains of Wentworth old church, comprising the west tower, the chancel and the north chapel, are all medieval. The old church was a chapel of ease for the township of Wentworth in the large parish of Wath, the parish church being 4 miles away. The earliest mention of the church was in 1235. Rebuilding took place in 1491 and again in 1548, this time with capitals and other materials brought from the dissolved Monk Bretton Priory. It was practically rebuilt by the 2nd Earl of Strafford in 1694. The square-headed windows have heraldry above and close examination of the tower reveals masons' marks. The upper parts of the tower fell down in the high winds of the great gale of 1962. The church is now in the care of the Churches Conservation Trust. The old church contains six memorials to the Wentworth family. One is a hanging wall monument to Sir William Wentworth (died 1614) and his wife Anne (died 1611), the two adults kneeling at a prayer desk. Sir William is wearing his best suit of armour. Below the parents, in the part of the monument called the predella, are their eleven children, boys on the left and girls on the right. The eldest son, Thomas Wentworth, the future 1st Earl of Strafford, is shown much bigger than the other children. Another monument is of Thomas Wentworth (died 1587) and his wife Margaret, in the form of two alabaster figures on a tomb chest of marble. They wear their best ruffs and their heads rest on braided tasselled pillows.

The last service in the old church took place on Sunday evening, 29 July 1877. The new church, Holy Trinity, was consecrated on Tuesday, 31 July 1877 by the Archbishop of York. It is in the Gothic Revival style, designed by one of the leading Victorian exponents of that style, John Loughborough Pearson. It was built in memory of the 5th Earl Fitzwilliam and his wife by their children. Its spire rises to 200 feet and can be seen for miles around. It was designed to seat a congregation of 540. Sir Nicholas Pevsner, the eminent architectural historian, said, 'the Fitzwilliams of the day could not have spent their money more judiciously.' In the church the altar is backed by a reredos carved in stone depicting the last supper. The roof is rib-vaulted and the nave is separated from the aisles by pillars carved as clusters of tree trunks. The great east window, showing scenes from the life of Christ, is by Clayton and Bell, and was completed in 1888 in memory of Admiral the Hon. George Henry Douglas, agent to the 6th Earl Fitzwilliam.

There are two public houses in the village, the Rockingham Arms and the George & Dragon. The name Rockingham Arms relates to the title adopted by Thomas Watson-Wentworth when he became 1st Marquis of that name in 1746. His grandmother, who was the sister of the 2nd Earl of Strafford, was Lady Rockingham of Rockingham Castle, in Northamptonshire. The same name was given to the family's pottery at Swinton, and to their colliery at Birdwell. The main building probably dates from the eighteenth century. The George & Dragon building is probably of seventeenth-century date, when it was not a public house but a private dwelling; it has been a public house since the eighteenth century. Manorial courts were once held there. The space in front of the George & Dragon was used in the past as a village marketplace. Both the George & Dragon and the Rockingham Arms were officially not open for business on Sundays until the 1970s, originally on the orders of the 5th Earl Fitzwilliam (1783–1858).

Almost opposite the Rockingham Arms on Main Street is the Mechanics' Institute, which was built in the early 1820s on the orders of Viscount Milton, who succeeded as the 5th Earl Fitzwilliam in 1833. It was among the first of such institutions to be formed in the country. It originally had a library and was designed as a meeting place and educational venue for working men as an alternative to the public house. The library has now gone but it still performs a broad educational role as the village hall. Just down Main Street from the Mechanics' Institute is a most attractive group of cottages situated

**The Mechanics' Institute, Wentworth.** *Pauline & Michael Bentley*

**Paradise Square in Wentworth village.**

round a central, beautifully tended garden area. This is Paradise Square, which was not originally built as a residential area but a farm, and the farmhouse, barns and other outhouses were converted to residential use. The former farm fold yard (farmyard) now forms the central area of gardens.

The Roundhouse in Clayfield Lane was one of three windmills once known to have stood in the Wentworth area. It was probably the 'new wind miln' built in 1745, recorded by the 1st Marquis of Rockingham. In July of that year, payment was made for 158,000 bricks, and the Roundhouse is made from handmade bricks. By 1793, it was no longer a working windmill and was converted into a cottage called the Saxon Tower. This is probably when the castellated top to the old windmill was added. There is another former windmill just beyond the other end of the village. This former windmill, along Mill Lane to the west of Wentworth, is now a private residence. The present structure was built in 1793 at a cost of £382-9s-1¼d. Beside the stone-built mill, a house, barn and stables were constructed for the miller and his family. By 1824, the windmill had been replaced by a steam-powered mill. Throughout most of the nineteenth century, one family of millers, the Jacksons, lived at the mill.

## Wentworth in 1851

It is interesting to analyse the population make-up of the village during the period when Wentworth was purely an estate village and when the Fitzwilliam family was in residence at the mansion. In 1851, the village from West Hall Fold at the western end to Hague Lane in the east, i.e. along Main Street from one end to the other, had a population of 548. And unlike Elsecar (see below), there was a real mixture of occupations. There were seven tenant farmers (including two widows), occupying land ranging from 7 acres to 95 acres, with their farmhouses on Main Street. There were also master craftsmen who worked for the Earl, including Joseph Falding, the master carpenter, who was in charge of twenty-five workers, and Francis Falding, the wood agent, in charge of ten workers. Seventeen gardeners who worked for the estate were also living in the village. The building trades (carpenters, joiners, plumbers and stone masons) were well represented, forty-one in all, many probably working directly on behalf of the estate. There was the usual mixture of other occupations found in any thriving Victorian community, such as blacksmith, cordwainer (i.e. a boot and shoemaker), a grocer and draper, a confectioner, a butcher, a saddler, eight tailors and two tailor's apprentices, and two innkeepers (Joseph Johnston at the George & Dragon and Maria Tyne at the Rockingham Arms). Also living in the village were John Levett, the curate of Wentworth, James Upton, the rector of Tankersley, and three school mistresses. Less expected residents were a retired gentleman's servant, a Chelsea Pensioner and a linen weaver. Females employed in addition to the two widowed farm tenants were thirty house servants, seven dressmakers and a straw hat maker. One female inhabitant was said to be the 'proprietor of houses'. Nine inhabitants were described as annuitants or paupers.

Living just outside the main village cluster on Clayfield Lane was Erasmus Stone, apothecary, surgeon and general practitioner. In the same household were a son, who was a veterinary surgeon, and another son, who was a medical student. One of Dr Stone's duties was the care of estate workers who had sustained work injuries. A little further outside the village, on Cortworth Lane at Chesnut Cottage lived Benjamin Biram, the Earl's colliery superintendant.

There were only seven coal miners (who would have worked at Elsecar), seven ironstone miners (who would have worked at bell pits in Tankersley Park) and nine employed at an ironworks (Elsecar or Milton) living in Wentworth in 1851. One of these Wentworth-based ironstone miners in 1851 was William Jubb, who was the undertaker at one of the twelve ironstone bell pits in Tankersley Park. An undertaker undertook to 'get' the ironstone in his pit, 'hurry' it to the bottom of the shaft and then lift it to the surface.[1] Jubb's team consisted of himself and a near neighbour as getters, a 16-year-old boy as a hurrier and a 14-year-old gin boy (the son of a neighbour), who would have been in charge of a pony operating a gin (a pulley system) used to lower the getters and the hurrier down the pit and to lift ironstone out of the pit. At the beginning and end of every working day they would have had a 2-mile walk to or from their workplace.

Three hundred and twenty-five of the inhabitants of the village in 1851 (59 per cent) had been born in Wentworth itself and 160 (29 per cent) had been born in surrounding towns and villages. Of the forty-nine long-distance migrants, the ones most distant from their birthplace were the Infant School mistress (from Scotland), three gardeners (also from Scotland), the assistant Infant School mistress (from Hastings, in Sussex), the Tankersley curate, his widowed mother and his sister (all from Middlesex), and the Chelsea Pensioner (from Buckinghamshire). There was also a small number of migrants who had probably once worked on the Earl's Northamptonshire estates (eleven individuals gave their birthplace as Northamptonshire), and one blacksmith's niece's birthplace was recorded as Grosvenor Square, where the Earl's London residence was located.

### Elsecar Collieries

In contrast to Wentworth village is Elsecar – physically just over a mile away but in location and conception almost the complete opposite of Wentworth. Whereas Wentworth was and still is surrounded on three sides by farmland and woodland, and on the fourth side by the entrance to Wentworth Park, Elsecar was developed next to a large colliery and an ironworks. The only thing they have in common is the use of the same building material – the mellow Coal Measures sandstone. Although we know that small coal pits were being worked near the outcrop of the Barnsley seam near the western edge of Hoyland Nether township in the seventeenth century,[2] the first detailed records of coal mining at Elsecar date from the eighteenth century. These relate to Low Wood Colliery and Elsecar Colliery. The first record of Low Wood Colliery is 1723. Elsecar Colliery was first mentioned in 1750. Both collieries worked the Barnsley seam near its outcrop, the pits sunk for Elsecar Colliery being no more than 16 yards (15 metres) deep. The seam was 9 feet thick. From the early 1750s, both collieries were under the estate's direct control. These were small collieries with, in the 1760s and early 1770s, only five men working underground at Elsecar Colliery and seven at Low Wood. Both collieries were distant from navigable water and yet in the second half of the eighteenth century they had surprisingly large market areas. This can be gauged from debt lists for the two collieries that survive for the 1762–88 period.[3] If customers in one area were no more likely to incur bad debts than people in another area, then the lists are very instructive. The markets for Elsecar coal were more local than those for Low Wood coal. They stretched north-eastwards into an area where there were no rival collieries, the route crossing the river Dearne towards the Magnesian Limestone escarpment and the lowlands beyond. The market for Low Wood coal stretched in the same direction but also included lowland areas further east extending into Nottinghamshire and Lincolnshire. Transport for Elsecar coal was all by horse-drawn wagon but Low Wood coal was transported by cart 5 miles (8 kilometres) to the estate wharf on the river Don at Kilnhurst, where it could be transported on the canalised river to markets on the lower Don and Trent.

The presence of the thick Barnsley seam and other seams – principally the Silkstone Seam and the Parkgate Seam – that could be reached from deep pits, together with improving transport links by canal and railway, and the expanding ironworks on the estate, all contributed to the vast expansion of the coal mining industry in and around Elsecar from the late eighteenth century onwards. The Act of Parliament for constructing the Dearne and Dove Canal along 9 miles of the Dearne Valley with cuts to Elsecar and Worsbrough received Parliamentary sanction in 1793, and the Elsecar branch was completed by 1796 as far as Cobcar Ings. By 1799, it had been extended to Elsecar, where a new colliery, Elsecar New Colliery, was sunk. There were three shafts at the new colliery, two coal-winding shafts and one pumping shaft. The pumping shaft was powered by a Newcomen-type engine, which has survived to the present day virtually intact, and in situ, and is a Scheduled Ancient Monument. Not only was there a new colliery at Elsecar but the workings at the old Elsecar Colliery were extended, and by 1850 there were three Elsecar collieries: Elsecar High Colliery (the Old Elsecar Colliery), Elsecar Mid Colliery (formerly Elsecar New Colliery, with a new shaft at Jump), and Elsecar Low Colliery at Hemingfield, just inside Wombwell township. Both the Mid Colliery and the shaft of the New Colliery at Jump were connected by inclined planes to the canal. In 1851, all three of these collieries were

**Elsecar Main Colliery.** *Chris Sharp*

The Newcomen Engine in Elsecar.

connected to the railway system when a branch line of the Dearne Valley route of the South Yorkshire Railway was built to a goods station at Elsecar. These collieries were superseded in 1853 by the sinking of a new colliery, Simon Wood Colliery, whose shaft reached the Barnsley seam at 93 yards. This colliery was in production for almost half a century before closing in 1903. It was superseded by Elsecar Main Colliery in 1908, designed initially to exploit the Parkgate Seam at 344 yards. Elsecar Main Colliery closed in 1983.

### The Elsecar and Milton Ironworks
There were two ironworks in Hoyland township; one at Elsecar itself and the other just to the north-west at Milton. The Elsecar Ironworks, located near the canal terminus, was opened in 1795 and leased to John Darwin and Company, who operated it until 1827 when Darwin went bankrupt. It was then operated by managers directly on behalf of Earl Fitzwilliam until 1848. Meanwhile, the Milton Ironworks, between Hoyland village and Elsecar, was established sometime from 1799 to 1802. It was leased by the Walkers of Masbrough until 1821 and then by Hartop, Sorby and Littlewood from 1821 to 1824. Hartop was Henry Hartop, from Sheffield, where his father operated the Park Ironworks. When Hartop's partners withdrew in 1824, he went into partnership with the Graham brothers, who invested £30,000 into the business. Hartop withdrew in 1829 and the Graham brothers operated alone until 1848. In June 1848, the Milton Ironworks was advertised to be let and the 5th Earl Fitzwilliam also decided to lease the Elsecar Ironworks. In 1849, a tenancy agreement was signed with George and William Henry Dawes, the sons of John Dawes, an ironmaster who ran the Bromford Ironworks in West Bromwich, in the Black Country of Staffordshire. During the Dawes's tenancy, besides blast furnaces there were puddling workshops (where pig iron was converted into wrought iron), rolling mills, fitting shops and foundries at the two works. George Dawes gave up the Elsecar and Milton operations at the end of 1884 on the opening of his Trent Ironworks at Scunthorpe. The Milton Ironworks became an iron and brass foundry. The Elsecar Ironworks was partly demolished and the rest converted into a series of estate maintenance workshops. It now houses the Elsecar Heritage Centre.

### Housing and amenities in Elsecar
The development of the colliery and ironworks and their related employment opportunities led to a population explosion and related settlement expansion. Elsecar grew from being a small hamlet around Elsecar Green into an estate industrial village. It survives largely intact to this day, a testament to the high quality of the housing provided. The oldest surviving working men's houses at Elsecar are the fifteen stone cottages that make up Old Row, which date from about 1795. The ten cottages on Station Row were built in about 1800, probably based on designs by John Carr, the York architect, who was employed on various schemes at that time by the 4th Earl Fitzwilliam. The longest row at Elsecar is Reform Row, consisting of twenty-eight cottages constructed in 1837. The two attractive rows that make up Cobcar Terrace were built about 1860.

**Old Row, Elsecar.**

In 1845, the Mines Commissioner Seymour Tremenheere described in some detail the housing provided for the miners at Elsecar.[4] He said their houses were 'of a class superior in size and arrangement and in the conveniences attached, to those belonging to the working classes'. He went to say that: 'Those at Elsecar consist of four rooms and a pantry, a small back court, ash-pit, a pig-sty and garden.' 'The gardens', he said, 'were cultivated with much care.' He pointed out the neatness of the front of each cottage, saying that the 'small space before the front door is walled round, and kept neat with flowers or paving stones; a low gate preventing children from straying into the road'. He also noted the 'conveniences, attached to every six or seven houses', which, he said, 'were kept perfectly clean'. He said that the village presented 'a remarkable contrast with the degrading neglect of cleanliness in person, house and habits, exhibited in so many of the colliery villages of Scotland'.

Besides the housing, Elsecar was also provided with Holy Trinity Church in 1843, at the expense of the 5th Earl Fitzwilliam, and the neighbouring school was built in 1852 to replace an earlier school. The village had street lighting from 1857 and a market hall was opened in 1870. In 1853, even a miners' lodging house was

**The former Miners' Lodging House, Elsecar.**

opened that accommodated twenty-two single men and contained the first indoor bath in Elsecar! It later became a police station and is now apartments. Almost the whole village of Elsecar is now a conservation area, with Old Row, Station Row, Reform Row, Cobcar Terrace and the former miners' lodging house all Grade 2 listed buildings.

### Elsecar in 1851

It is revealing, when the census enumerator's returns are analysed, to see the exact make-up of the population of Elsecar when it had become a fully fledged industrial village. What proportion of the working men and boys were coal miners? Did son follow father into the pit? Were the adults mainly local or were there medium- and long-distance migrants living there? In 1851, for example, the population of Elsecar was 557, which included 185 working men and boys. Of these working men and boys, 102 (55 per cent) were coal miners and fifteen (8 per cent) worked in the ironworks. What this means is that in 1851, Elsecar was not just an industrial village but emphatically a mining village. In Reform Row, the longest of the rows of cottages in the village, containing twenty-eight dwellings, of the fifty working men and boys, forty-three (86 per cent) were coal miners. And this concentration of coal miners was in complete contrast to the area called Stubbin, immediately to the north-west of Elsecar, and the area around Milton Ironworks, where the vast majority of working men and boys were ironworkers. It is said that the Fitzwilliams were reluctant to employ workers from beyond the estate who were not familiar with the working arrangements in their collieries and whose background and character were unknown.[5] For this reason, the relatives of existing employees were preferred. This is borne out by the 1851 census. In many of the Elsecar mining families not only were the fathers employed as colliers, but so were their sons and other family relatives such as sons-in-law and brothers-in-law. The youngest workers in 1851 were a coal miner aged 12 and a moulder's apprentice aged 10.

Besides the coal miners and ironworks workers and their families there was the usual mix of families headed by persons in other types of employment found in all busy and thriving settlements. At Elsecar in 1851, these included: a curate, the Reverend George Scaife; a schoolmaster, Edward Quick; Earl Fitzwilliam's coal agent, Joshua Cooper; a corn miller, Joshua Jackson; and a coal shipping agent, James Uttley. There were also a shopkeeper, a tailor, a shoemaker, a butcher, two innkeepers and surprisingly, two men employed in the gardens at Wentworth Woodhouse. Females employed included house servants, dressmakers, seamstresses and one charwoman.

For the reasons outlined above, it is not surprising to find that most of the inhabitants of Elsecar in 1851 were locally born. Thirty-three per cent of the inhabitants had been born in Elsecar itself, 63 per cent had been born in the surrounding local area – mostly neighbouring villages such as Wentworth, Thorpe Hesley, Scholes, Greasbrough, Wombwell and Worsbrough – and only 4 per cent were from more distant parts of Yorkshire or other counties. In Reform Row, the local origins of the inhabitants were even more marked: sixty-three had been born in Elsecar itself, 103 in surrounding settlements and only two from further afield – a head of household (a miner) who had born in Nottingham and the wife of a miner who had been born in Preston in Lancashire. It should also be noted that, in complete contrast, in the area around the Milton Ironworks, at Stubbin and in Hoyland village, there were 204 migrants who had been born in the West Midland counties who had migrated north to join the incoming ironmasters, the Dawes brothers, in 1849.[6]

In addition to the permanent population of Elsecar, on census day in 1851 there were also twenty people on barges in the canal basin. The heads of the families were referred to as 'Captain' or 'Boatman'. Not surprisingly, in that a major domestic market for household coal lay in the areas to the east beyond the working coalfield, their birthplaces included a number on the lower Don or Humber at places such as Stainforth, Fishlake, Thorne and Lincolnshire Bridge.

## Elsecar by the Sea

In the early twentieth century, Elsecar gained another reputation. It became a popular destination for those wanting a day out at the 'seaside': it became known as Elsecar by the Sea. It all started in 1910 when a local barber and amateur photographer,

Herbert Parkin, sent some photographs of Elsecar reservoir to the *Sheffield Star* that were published under the title 'Elsecar-by-the-Sea'. The reservoir, built to feed the canal, together with its neighbouring park, became a Mecca for local day trippers for decades. Visitors from local villages were joined by people from Sheffield and Barnsley who could come by train and get off at the nearby Elsecar & Hoyland railway station. There was a large artificial beach where you could paddle, swim or boat, and you could even buy Elsecar rock! And Water Lane, which runs beside the reservoir, became known as the Promenade. A full range of picture postcards was also on sale to visitors.

*Chapter 8*

# THE FAMILY'S PATERNALISTIC CONCERN FOR THEIR EMPLOYEES AND TENANTS

The Fitzwilliams, as well as providing employment, also supplied home comforts, education and health care. They built houses, churches and schools for their workers, and they erected estate almshouses, gave pensions to widows, employed doctors to look after the health of their employees, and much more. They were not unique in their attitude to their employees and tenants but they were certainly outstanding and unusual, not only in their caring approach but also in the longevity of that standpoint over generations. The 4th and 5th Earls Fitzwilliam, for example, were described by Graham Mee in his book *Aristocratic Enterprise* as 'archetypes of the paternalist for whom the poor were indeed children to be cared for and controlled in a fatherly manner'.[1]

### St Thomas's Day and Collop Monday

Their benevolent attitude to their workers is well exemplified by their stance with regard to the St Thomas's Day and Collop Monday traditions. St Thomas's Day falls on 21 December, the winter solstice, the shortest day and the longest night of the year. On that day, also called Thomassing Day, Mumping Day, Gooding Day and Corning Day, poor people begged money and provisions for Christmas. Farmers often added a measure of corn to the gleaners' pickings from the autumn and winter fields, and this was ground free of charge in some places by the local miller. Collop Monday was part of Shrovetide, which also included Egg Saturday, Quinquagesima Sunday and Shrove Tuesday (Pancake Day). Collop Monday was a day of games and dancing, and feasts to consume the food that was forbidden during Lent. Sidney Oldall Addy, in his supplement to his *Sheffield Glossary* in 1891, links the Collop Monday and Shrove Tuesday customs thus: 'On this day poor people go to their richer neighbours to beg a collop or slice of bacon, to supply the fat in which pancakes are baked on the following day.'[2]

St Thomas's Day and Collop Monday were formalised and institutionalised on the South Yorkshire Wentworth estate in the nineteenth century by successive Earls

**Outdoor employees queuing for the St Thomas's Day donation.** *Eric Leslie*

Fitzwilliam. Outdoor employees (those in the mansion had separate arrangements) were given a quantity of beef and a sum of money (sixpence in the 1840s) on St Thomas's Day and beef and bacon on Collop Monday. They had to be regular employees rather than those doing occasional jobs. It is not clear when the customs in their nineteenth-century form originated or when they ceased to operate, but they were recorded as early as 1788, and detailed records have survived in the Wentworth Woodhouse Muniments in Sheffield Archives for the periods 1811–28 and 1841–56, in the time of the 4th Earl Fitzwilliam (who succeeded to the Wentworth estates in 1782 and died in 1833) and the 5th Earl (who succeeded in 1833 and died in 1857).[3]

The operation of the two charities was a massive undertaking. In 1841, for example, there were just over 1,000 recipients. The largest group consisted of coal miners: 181 at Elsecar and Jump Colliery, 168 at Elsecar Old Colliery, 126 at Parkgate Colliery, 55 at Strafford Colliery and 54 at Stubbin Colliery. Twenty-four maintenance men at the Tankersley ironstone grounds were also included (the miners themselves at this date were considered self-employed and were excluded), together with 12 men constructing the Thorncliffe Drift, a major mine drainage project stretching from Elsecar to Thorncliffe. Other groups of employees included in the 1841 distributions were 54 workers at Elsecar Ironworks, 65 building the 'Greasbro New Coach Road', 40 carpenters, 35 masons, 8 sawyers, 6 joiners and 4 plumbers. The agricultural land and estate woodlands provided 85 workers and the park and gardens 87 workers, including 6 working at the menagerie, a 'boat tenter' at the lakes, a rat-catcher and a stable bed maker! In addition, 12 former employees were listed who were residents at the hospital (almshouses) in Wentworth village.

In 1841, the beef distributed amounted to 439 stones (2,788 kilograms) from five bulls. Everyone had to turn up personally and names were ticked off lists drawn up by heads of departments. St Thomas's Day and succeeding days must have been times of plenty in those households where the husband and several sons were all Fitzwilliam estate workers. And the same list of employees was used the following March on Collop Monday. The length of the list of recipients grew and grew. In 1850, for example, there were 1,232, including 606 coal miners and all 271 ironstone miners working in Tankersley Park and at Skiers Spring.

### The Irish Famine and the 5th Earl Fitzwilliam's response

From 1845 to 1851, potato crops – the staple food of many small tenant farmers in Ireland – were devastated by blight. Starvation was rife, killing an estimated one million people during those years. There was also an epidemic of typhus, from which 350,000 died in 1846 and 1847. Survivors could not pay their rents, many were evicted, and large-scale emigration – notably to England, Scotland, Canada and the USA – took place.

The Fitzwilliam estate in County Wicklow was not exempt from this great catastrophe. But what must be emphasised is that the poorest inhabitants of the estate, and therefore those most susceptible to crop failure, starvation, disease and inability to pay their rent, were mostly not direct tenants of the Earl. As on other estates throughout Ireland at that time, absentee landlords like Earl Fitzwilliam let substantial farms to Protestant chief tenants who, in turn, whether or not they themselves were resident, sublet parts to subtenants (often referred to as middlemen). Chief tenants and middlemen would then let parts of their farms to cottiers, mostly Catholic, who lived in small cabins, cultivated potato patches and kept milk cows. If possible, they paid their rents through labouring for their tenant landlord. But even before the potato blight struck there were always more labourers seeking work than there was work available. It was, therefore, the cottiers and their families who suffered most during the famine. Three examples of families of cottiers on the Fitzwilliam estate illustrate what would have been their parlous situation as the famine began to rage.

> The Balf family living in 1847 at Hillbrook near the estate village of Carnew: consisting of father and mother, five children aged fourteen to three months. They lived in a cabin, and had a kitchen garden rented from Mr Shannon, a tenant of Mr Symes who was the chief tenant who paid his rent to the Fitzwilliam estate.
>   The Loughnan family living in 1848 at Coollattin, consisting of mother and father and eight children aged eighteen to three months. They rented a cabin and kitchen garden from Mr Sherwood.
>   The Fox family living in 1849 at Coolboy near the estate village of Carnew, consisting of mother and father, nine children aged twenty-six to seven, and a son-in-law and his two-year old daughter. They rented a tiny piece of land three roods and twenty-seven perches in size [i.e. just less than an acre (0.4 hectares)] from Earl Fitzwilliam.[4]

The onset of the potato blight in 1845 in County Wicklow was not considered a disaster as it had happened before, but in 1846, the potato crop was almost completely destroyed. With their inability to harvest their own main food crop, agricultural labouring opportunities in steep decline and consequently a great shortage of money to purchase food supplies, starvation and illness among the poorest sections of the population rose steeply. Under the Poor Law (Ireland) Act of 1838, five workhouses were erected in County Wicklow, including one in Shillelagh at the centre of the Fitzwilliam estate. It was built to accommodate 400 paupers. In addition, a scheme of relief work projects such as road building and improvements, and land drainage schemes, had been put in place to provide work opportunities to enable the poorest to earn money to buy alternative food supplies. By the winter of 1846/47, the Shillelagh workhouse was full to overflowing, soup kitchens were in operation and the poor but able-bodied men were earning money to buy food by labouring on the relief work schemes.

It was at this point that Earl Fitzwilliam, through his Irish land agent Robert Chaloner, greatly expanded a scheme that had been in operation for a number of years – assisted emigration to Canada.[5] And unlike on many large Irish estates where poor cottiers were simply evicted, the Fitzwilliam emigration scheme was a voluntary one: the head of each family had to apply to emigrate and they were given assistance to do so. Information about those families wishing to emigrate was collected by senior estate employees and recorded in emigration books.

It has been estimated that from 1847 to 1856, approximately 850 families (more than 6,000 people) whose heads were Fitzwilliam tenants or tenants of middlemen on the Fitzwilliam Wicklow estate emigrated to Canada with direct help from the Earl. Their applications to migrate were listed in the estate emigration books, which still survive and from which the information about the Balf, Loughnan and Fox families quoted above is taken. Successful applicants were given a small sum of money when they quit their tenanted land, with additional payments for crops they had planted and their manure heaps, and if their cabins were taken down and the materials used elsewhere. Clothing and provisions allowances were available, and each family got a chest, handcrafted by local carpenters, in which to store their belongings on the voyage, and, if necessary, a cart on which to carry their belongings and the very young and old to the port of embarkation. They embarked at New Ross, 60 miles away in County Wexford. The able-bodied had to walk there; it took three days.

The first ships sailed in April 1847, carrying more than 2,000 men, women and children. Earl Fitzwilliam had arranged for William Graves & Company to provide the emigration ships. The first ship to sail, on 12 April, was the *Dunbrody*, carrying 317 passengers. The Canadian coast was reached on 18 May, at which point there had been five deaths on board. They then sailed up the St Lawrence River to the city of Quebec, but before they could set foot there they had to spend ten days at a quarantine centre on Grosse Isle, an island in the river. This must have been an horrific experience for those emigrants who had been spared illness on the voyage. The conditions on Grosse Isle were dreadful, and became progressively worse as more emigrant ships

**A village priest blesses Irish emigrants as they leave home for a port.** *Illustrated London News, 10 May 1851*

arrived from Europe, with many cases of dysentery and typhus. Fortunately, because of the small number of deaths during the voyage, the passengers on the *Dunbrody* were cleared from quarantine after three days.

In 1847, more than 2,000 Fitzwilliam emigrants entered Canada and emigration via the St Lawrence River continued, with dwindling numbers, until 1856, when there were only four assisted emigrant families. But in 1849, an additional destination was arranged: Earl Fitzwilliam organised for 100 men to be supplied for three months for the building of a new railway from the port of St Andrews in New Brunswick northwards, just north of the border with the United States, to the city of Quebec. The Earl footed the wages bill. However, in addition to the 100 able-bodied workmen, the agent also sent their families, amounting altogether to 380 people. They sailed in the *Star* in late April 1849. Nine people died en route. After landing at what was called 'Hospital Island', fever broke out and there was much illness and death. Accommodation for the fit workers and their families was in very short supply because neither the railway company nor the town authorities, nor even the province of New Brunswick, had expected so many emigrants. The railway project was a failure. Many of the emigrants stayed in New Brunswick; others left for other parts of eastern Canada, and some crossed into the state of Maine in the USA.

The question naturally arises: were the 5th Earl and his Irish land agent intransigent cleaners-up of the estate, wishing to rid themselves of 'surplus people', or were they sympathetic and generous paternalists looking to the best interests of the poor and starving? There can be no doubt that their motives and their approach were much more empathetic, humane and financially generous than many other Irish absentee landlords. The emigrants were voluntary, not forced migrants. And although it can only be concluded that the 5th Earl's assisted emigration scheme was of mixed success, the vast majority of the assisted emigrants not only survived, but they and their descendants went on to lead successful lives in their new homelands.[5]

### The care of employees, the young, the elderly, the widowed and the sick

Provision was made from childhood until old age, not only for employees but also directly through schools and local charities for tenants and other members of the local population living on the family's estates throughout England and Ireland. And it was not just a general paternalism; individual cases were considered and action taken. Day schools, Sunday schools and churches were built at the family's expense. The churches and schools in Wentworth village and Elsecar have already been referred to (see Chapter 7) but they were also active elsewhere. For example, in South Yorkshire, the 4th Earl Fitzwilliam was a major contributor to the building costs of St Mary's church at Greasbrough, and the 6th Earl gave the land for the building of St Thomas's church at Kilnhurst, near Swinton. Also, let us not forget the four new churches and four new schools that were built, and repairs to ten churches that were undertaken on the Irish estate in the early eighteenth century that are referred to in Chapter 2.

The family also took especial care of those in the most profitable but also most dangerous part of the estate's economy: its collieries, which for two centuries provided a very substantial estate income. They were blessed by a succession of outstanding mining superintendants, none more so than father and son Joshua and Benjamin Biram. Joshua Biram took over this responsibility from his uncle, Benjamin Hall, who died in 1805, and Joshua was in charge of the collieries until he retired in 1833. His son, Benjamin, whose talents were spotted at an early age, was privately educated at the 4th Earl Fitzwilliam's expense at the Bluecoat School in London. He became his father's clerk and assistant in 1823 and took over the reins on Joshua's retirement. During Benamin's term of office, which ended with his early death at the age of 53 in 1857, employment at the estate's South Yorkshire collieries rose from just over 300 to more than 850. And as the collieries got deeper, and the workings underground expanded, the danger from flooding and gas explosions increased. In his book on nineteenth-century South Yorkshire mining disasters, local mining historian Brian Elliott lists twenty-one mining disasters, with fatalities amounting to 973. One of these incidents, which took the lives of ten miners, occurred in 1852 at the estate's Elsecar Low Colliery at Hemingfield, near Wombwell.[6] Ten fatalities out of 973 for the region as a whole is a small figure, but even ten is ten too many.

It is generally believed that the pits under Benjamin Biram's supervision were among the safest at that time. He invented an anemometer to measure the flow of air through the mine workings, as well as an underground fan to improve ventilation and an advanced miner's lamp that gave off four times the amount of light of a Davy lamp. And such was his expertise that he was invited to give evidence to a select committee of the House of Lords in 1849 on the best means of preventing dangerous accidents in coal mines. He was questioned at length and explained how and why he had invented an anemometer, a fan and an improved miners' lamp. Such was the esteem in which he was held by the Elsecar miners that they presented him with a silver cup in 1856 at a ceremony held in the Elsecar workshops, which was attended by hundreds of miners and

**A replica of Benjamin Biram's safety lamp on display in Elsecar Heritage Centre Museum.**

Hanging wall monument in Wentworth old church. Sir William Wentworth (died 1614) and his wife Anna (died 1611) are kneeling at a prayer desk. Below them are their eleven children, divided by gender. The largest figure is their eldest son, Thomas, who became the 1st Earl of Strafford.

Interior of St John the Baptist church, Hooton Roberts, thought to be a possible burial place for the 1st Earl of Strafford.

Thomas Watson-Wentworth. (James Saunders Watson of Rockingham Castle)

The library at Trinity College, Dublin, built using timbers from the Watson-Wentworth estate woodlands. (Kevin Lee)

The Baroque (west) front of Wentworth Woodhouse, built from 1724 to 1732.

Harrowden Hall, Northamptonshire.

Portrait of Charles, who became 2nd Marquis of Rockingham, and his sister, Charlotte. The inclusion of the bullfinch reminds viewers that their mother's maiden name was Finch.

The 2nd Marquis of Rockingham's portrait. The original was painted by Joshua Reynolds.

Mill Dam in Wentworth Park, looking towards Greasbrough church.

A Japanese maple in autumn colours, and the remains of the duck houses.

The replica 'famine ship', *Dunbrody*. (Dunbrody Trust)

Elsecar church.

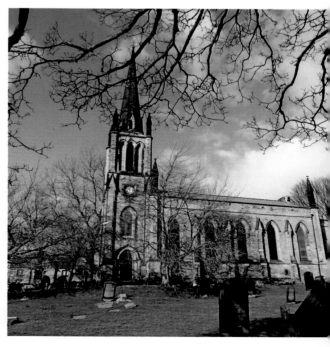

The Marble Saloon in Wentworth Woodhouse, with some of the statues described by Joseph Woodcock.

The 6th Earl Fitzwilliam out hunting. Shown left to right are: Lady Albreda Fitzwilliam, George Ireton, Lady Alice Fitzwilliam, 6th Earl Fitzwilliam and Frank Bartlett.
(Taken from an oil print by John Baxter belonging to Joan Swann)

WENTWORTH WOODHOUSE

Allan Womersl.

The Palladian (east) front of Wentworth Woodhouse, painted by Allan Womersley. (Ena Womersley)

The recently restored Long Gallery.

their wives. In his address, a miner, Samuel Thornsby spoke of 'the great comfort and advantages we enjoy in having placed over us a gentleman of so much kindness, ability and intelligence as yourself, we have thought well to show our gratitude for such a blessing bestowed upon us by Divine Providence'.[7]

At a time long before the National Health Service, when employers may or may not have had any paternal concern for their sick, injured or retired employees and tenants and their families, the Fitzwilliams did their utmost to provide care and financial assistance. For example, if an injury occurred at work, and therefore an employee could no longer earn his or her wages, these were often continued or a monetary allowance was made. Retired employees also received a small pension but, unless they were in any way disabled, estate workers laboured to a great age, so workers' pensions were relatively rare. There is a record of one estate labourer working until he was 93! In the first half of the nineteenth century a widow of an estate miner or a labourer in another estate department received a weekly pension of two shillings and sixpence, but if the widow had a large, young family, this could be raised to as high as seven shillings and sixpence. The widow's pension was even continued, at a reduced rate, if she remarried. It is also recorded that on at least two occasions, when a widow died, her pension continued to be paid to her children. By the time of the 5th Earl's death in 1857, there were nearly 100 weekly pensioners on the home estate.[8]

It has already been pointed out in Chapter 7 that a hospital (i.e. almshouses) was established at Barrow at the western end of Wentworth village in the early eighteenth century by Thomas Watson-Wentworth, in accordance with his uncle's (the 2nd Earl of Strafford) will. And the almshouses still operate today, run by a board of trustees of the Fitzwilliam Wentworth Estates Company. There were originally twelve dwellings but these have now been altered to house eight residents. It is interesting to identify the residents of the almshouses when the estate was in full operation with, for example, many house servants, coal miners, park keepers and gardeners in employment. At the time of the 1891 census, for example, eleven of the twelve dwellings were occupied. The occupants were six widows aged from 63 to 79 (one of whom had her 55-year-old daughter staying with her), three widowers aged from 69 to 85, and two married couples – one couple aged 72 and 74, and the other aged 65 and 67. The widows included Ann Steadman, whose late husband had been a forge labourer, and Catherine Greenwood, whose late husband had been a groom. James and Ann Raynor were one of the retired couples, James being a retired Elsecar coal miner. The other retired couple were Uriah and Susan Burgin, Uriah also a former miner who was listed as being 'much injured' in the 1852 explosion at Elsecar Low Colliery.[9]

This concern for estate employees, former employees and their families endured. On 13 March 1936, Geoffrey Steer, aged 14 years and 3 months, was due to leave Barrow School. His father had been killed in a mining accident and it was well known that Geoffrey did not want to work in a colliery. He was called to the headmaster's study and told to report to the head gardener, Mr Alex Third, on the following Monday morning. And so, as a teenager, he worked as a garden boy. His jobs included fetching milk from the Home Farm every morning for the fourteen gardeners who lived in the bothy, taking the rain gauge to Mr Third, and then washing plant pots till 11.30 am.

**Geoff Steer collecting cow manure for tomato fertiliser.** *Eric Leslie*

His next task was to light the fire in the gardeners' cabin to warm their tea bottles. And so it went on. His jobs also included fetching cow manure in a wheelbarrow from the fields beside Church Drive for making tomato fertiliser, and on two occasions he accompanied Mr Third to the mansion to replace the flower displays in the bedrooms. When they entered the mansion they had to take off their boots and find a pair of slippers of the right size.[10]

As well as the widows and their children, those suffering from work injuries, and pensioners and annuitants being cared for, they were also entertained. As described in detail in Chapter 10, whenever the family was celebrating a special occasion such as the completion of a building project, the succession to the estate, a wedding anniversary or the visit of a king, these people as well as the local population were included. But the family's generosity went much beyond that. Towards the end of the annual household accounts, stretching from the eighteenth to the twentieth century, there is a section entitled 'Bounties and Charities'. In the 1788 list, for example, there is a payment for Mr John Tyne (landlord of the Rockingham Arms) 'for Ale given to the Populace at Wentworth the 5th November', and another one to Mr John Parkin 'for Ale from the different Public Houses in Greasbro given to the Populace there Nov. 5th'. Obviously, Bonfire Night would have been much looked forward to. On 31 December in the same year, there is an entry for 'Thomas Turner Clerk of Wentworth Chapel a Christmas Box'.[11] More than a century later, the Bounties and Charities section of the household accounts lists subscriptions to a wide range of medical charities: Doncaster Royal Infirmary, Rotherham Hospital and Dispensary, Sheffield Royal Infirmary, Sheffield Children's Hospital, Jessop's Hospital in Sheffield, West London Hospital, Askern Baths Charity and the Sea-bathing Infirmary in Scarborough.[12] It also became usual at the two points in the year when tenants came to pay their half-yearly rents at the estate office that they stayed for a meal. In 1884, for example, 306, 467, 351 and 126 meals were served to tenants on Wednesday, Thursday, Friday and Saturday respectively in the second week of November. The tradition of a 'rent-feast' lasted until 1942, when due to food shortages and rationing, a small money payment was substituted.

**Walter Chapman (left) with his wooden arm poses with a lawn mower.** *Pat Swift*

It was not only the head of the family, through his senior estate staff, who dispensed charity and good works. Countess Maud (died 1967), wife of the 7th Earl, was well known for her charitable work. She was a supporter of the Painted Fabrics Limited, the organisation founded in Sheffield in 1923 to help to encourage and retrain soldiers, sailors and airmen who had been wounded and disabled in the First World War, and she was also a supporter of a charity that looked after the welfare of pit ponies. One day early last century, a boy, Walter Chapman, went to visit his father, who worked in the estate 'power house' (whose chimney still survives beside the Home Farm on Cortworth Lane, near the Octagon Lodge). There was an explosion and Walter lost his right arm. Countess Maud had been out with the Wentworth Hunt that day but she went to visit him in hospital, still in her hunting gear. She gave him the little brooch she always wore in the lapel of her hunting jacket and told him not to worry, and that there would always be a job for him on the estate. He became a much respected estate gardener, specialising in vegetable growing, and was said to 'pick peas quicker than anyone else'.

*Chapter 9*

# EARL FITZWILLIAM, COCOS ISLAND AND THE TREASURE OF LIMA

## Cocos Island and its legend

Prior to the opening of the Panama Canal in 1914, European explorers had to undertake a voyage of over 12,000 miles to reach Cocos Island, which is situated in the Gulf of Panama, in the Pacific Ocean. They were obliged to pass through the Strait of Magellan, at the tip of South America (so as to avoid Cape Horn). Nevertheless, some 300 expeditions to the island were undertaken from 1850 to 1978, when the Costa Rican government declared the entire island off limits. We may wonder why these travellers continued to set out, when the destination was so remote and difficult to explore, and when nothing of material value was ever found there, but readers of the *Peace Handbook 1920*, published by His Majesty's Stationery Office, were left in little doubt as to the answer:

> In 1818 or 1819 a notorious pirate known as Benito, alias Bennett Graham, [hid] a vast plunder he had obtained by rifling certain churches in Peru. A few years afterwards, it is said, Benito deposited a fresh quantity of gold bars and specie, worth eleven million dollars. In or about 1826 a man passing as William Thompson, who appears to have previously served under Benito, but was then in command of the brig *Mary Read*, concealed about twelve million dollars' worth of stolen gold coin, jewels, and silver ingots on Cocos Island.

Further, it was the official opinion of the British Civil Service that:

> The existence of treasure concealed in the island is well established and has been a matter of notoriety among residents not only of Costa Rica but of all the principal coast towns from Lima to Vancouver for many years.[1]

There were several legends about how there came to be treasure on Cocos Island, but the main one concerns the so-called 'Treasure of Lima'. There were three figures who were central to this story: Captain William Thompson, John Keating and

Nicholas (or Patrick?) Fitzgerald. So, we are told, the Treasure of Lima consisted of a vast reserve of gold and silver, which the Spaniards had accumulated in Lima but were unable to bring home because of the wars of independence in Central and South America. In 1821, when the army of the 'Liberator of Argentina', José de San Martín, was approaching the city, the Spanish viceroy supposedly entrusted the imperial treasure to a British trader, Captain William Thompson, so that he could convey it to a place of safety in his ship, the *Mary Dear* (or perhaps it was the *Mary Deer*, or even the *Mary Dier*?). But Thompson proved unreliable. Instead of following orders, he and his crew killed the Viceroy's men and sailed to Cocos Island, where they buried the loot. Shortly afterwards, they were arrested on the high seas by a Spanish warship and the whole crew (except Thompson and his first mate) were executed for piracy. In exchange for their lives, the two survivors promised to reveal where the treasure was hidden, but once they were put back on the island they ran off into the jungle, from where they eventually escaped, without the treasure. It is impossible to be sure where they hid it (assuming, of course, that there is any truth in the legend at all).

As he lay dying in Newfoundland twenty or more years later, Thompson passed his secret to John Keating, and supposedly, the latter made three voyages to Cocos Island. Twenty years later, Keating met another shady figure, whose surname was Fitzgerald. This fellow had retired from the sea and made no further voyages himself, but he passed the secret (and a map showing where the treasure was to be found) to the genuinely historical figure of Henry Palliser (1839–1907), an officer in the Royal Navy who, following various promotions, was appointed Commander-in-Chief of the Pacific Station in 1896. Palliser made one landing on Cocos Island while he was on duty in the Pacific, but we are told that he kept the secret to himself until he could find someone back home to fund a private expedition. In the end, he found a backer in the 7th Earl Fitzwilliam.

### The expedition
So it was that, on the morning of 21 October 1904, the former Union Castle 3,264 ton mail steamship *Harlech Castle* – converted into a private yacht and renamed the *Véronique* after a French musical that was on in Southampton at the time – slipped out of Southampton Water headed for the South Atlantic, South America and the Pacific via the Strait of Magellan. On board were the treasure party and a crew consisting of a captain, three officers, a doctor and nearly sixty men. No forwarding addresses were left behind; the expedition was a secret, masquerading at various times as a round-the-world pleasure cruise, a party prospecting for new coal reserves and a scientific plant-hunting expedition.

The treasure party – the Earl and seven of his friends and acquaintances – were a very mixed lot. The Earl, who had succeeded to the title in 1902, was in his early thirties and was described in one newspaper report as an 'intrepid sportsman, an adept mining engineer, a traveller, a cyclist, a polo player and a mighty hunter', and also had a distinguished military career, having served in the Boer War and been awarded the DSO. Other members of the party included: Admiral Palliser, who was in his early

The *Véronique.*

sixties, had served in the Crimean War and had retired in 1899; Mr St John Durnford, a mining engineer; Frank Brooke, the Earl's Irish estate agent; David T. Smith, the squire's son from Barnes Hall, near Grenoside, whose eldest brother had married the Earl's sister, Lady Mabel; George Eustace Cooke-Yarborough, who lived at Campsmount, at Campsall, near Doncaster; Captain North, 'Master of the Horse' at Wentworth Woodhouse; and a Mr Bulkeley. A small number of coal miners from the Earl's South Yorkshire collieries were also attached to the party. It is the journal of George Eustace Cooke-Yarborough and an article written by David T. Smith that form the basis of this account.[2]

They steamed southwards, stopping off at the Cape Verde islands to take on coal. While there they went fishing, using beef as bait, catching two red mullets and a conger eel, and Bulkeley bought a one-eyed white terrier, which caused trouble when it insisted on fighting the ship's cat! They were then refused entry to Rio de Janeiro because of civil unrest (the two political parties were settling whether to introduce a vaccination act by fighting it out in the streets). But an even more bizarre episode had occurred off the northern coast of Spain when a British cruiser asked them to alter course so that the British fleet could possibly get a shot or two at the Russian fleet, which was sailing from the Baltic to the Far East to take on the Japanese. After sailing 18,000 miles, all the Russian ships were sunk.

During the first week of the voyage the ship rolled badly in the rough weather in the Bay of Biscay and most of the party were horribly seasick, including the cow, which had to be taken on walks round the deck. It was a member of the party because, as David Smith remarked, 'Tinned milk did not appeal to some of the buccaneers'. The sea got calmer and the weather much warmer as they approached the tropics. Shoals of flying fish accompanied the yacht and the officers and crew turned out in white drill uniforms. They dropped anchor in the River Plate at Montevideo, Uruguay, on 15 November, where their arrival was announced in the *Montevideo Times* and they were treated royally, even being made honorary members of the English Club. Their claim that they were a scientific expedition exploring the tropics for minerals and rare orchids caused

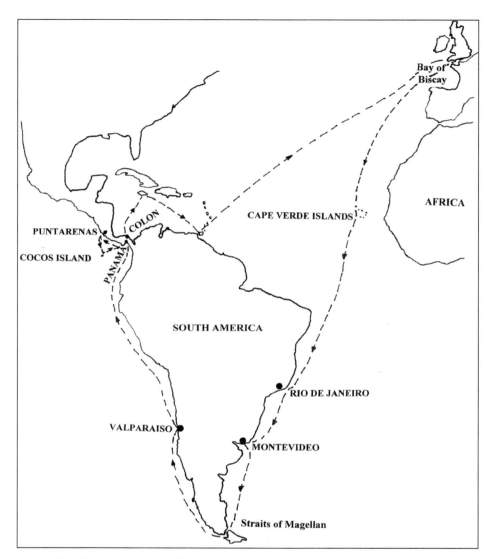

**A map showing the route taken by the adventurers.**

raised eyebrows. A number of the party went by steamer from Montevideo to Buenos Aires, Argentina, for a few days.

From Montevideo, they sailed with an expert pilot on board to negotiate the Strait of Magellan to enter the Pacific. The journey through the strait, on 25–29 November via Possession Bay, Fortesque Bay, Smyth's Channel and Trinidad Channel, was fascinating and exciting, with good views of penguins and seals – and even a Scotsman who worked as a trapper, was reputed to have five Tierra Fuegan wives, and hoisted the Union Jack

**Captain Bulkeley attends to the cow.** *Sir Anthony Cooke-Yarborough*

as they passed. In an inlet called Porto Bueno, they decided to go on a hunting trip to shoot deer, duck and geese for the larder. It was a disaster. They came back wet through and covered in slime. The only thing they killed was a cormorant, shot accidentally when a gun went off while they were getting out of their boat.

Once in the Pacific they turned north along the Chilean coast, heading for Valparaíso, Chile's chief port, more than 1,000 miles away. Heavy seas en route brought the return of seasickness among the party. They reached Valparaíso on 3 December. They were captivated by the town, which was built on steep ridges and described by one of the party as 'picturesque', with funicular railways connecting the harbour with the central part of the town. Their welcome in Valparaíso was even more rapturous than the one they had experienced in Montevideo. They were made members of the Naval Club by officers of the Chilean Navy and of the Union Club by the British residents, who also gave them a box at the opera. Again, as at Montevideo, their claim that they were a scientific expedition was greeted with some incredulity. Eventually, they left the port for a journey of 2,600 miles to Panama.

When they arrived at Panama after ten days' sailing they tied up next to an American cruiser. It should be pointed out that the Americans had been granted a 10-mile wide strip across the Isthmus of Panama in 1903 to construct the Panama Canal to connect the Atlantic with the Pacific Ocean, and so there was a strong American presence at Panama – something that came in very handy later on in the expedition. Yellow fever was raging in Panama when they arrived, and when they went ashore they bandaged their ankles and took strong doses of quinine. This was not thought necessary by some members of the crew of the American cruiser and six of them died within forty-eight hours. While tied up they indulged in some shark fishing even though they did not have the proper equipment. After a long struggle, in which a shark nearly dragged two of the party overboard, they managed to tie their line (a length of rope fastened to a short steel chain) around a winch and hauled the huge fish aboard, although they had to spring back and take cover as it lashed about the deck, 'snapping his jaws like an angry wolf', as David Smith described it.

From Panama, they sailed north on 19 December to Costa Rica, where they anchored at the port of Puntarenas. While at anchor they noticed a steam yacht with another treasure party aboard, led by a Mr Harold Gray, a well-known and wealthy sportsman, who informed them that they had already been to Cocos Island and had left a dozen men there digging for the treasure. He informed the Earl that he had obtained a concession from the Costa Ricans, giving him exclusive rights to search for the treasure. So Earl Fitzwilliam went with three other members of the party by train and mule to San José, the capital city, which lay inland in the mountains, at 4,000 feet. The reason for the visit was for an audience with the President in the hope that he would ratify the provisional permission that had been given by the Costa Rican ambassador in Paris for them to land on Cocos Island and search for the treasure.

While this diplomatic mission was away, some members of the treasure party, accompanied by some of the ship's crew and the miners attached to the party, went on several hunting expeditions around the coastal islands, where they shot an armadillo and stalked an alligator. One day, they took a launch and linked up with an American known as 'Mr Max' and visited the governor of a penal colony on St Luke's Island. The Governor invited them for breakfast … but the British did not know what they had let themselves in for. Apparently, the Governor had killed a suckling pig 'expressly for their delectation' and he allowed them to refuse nothing. The breakfast consisted of macaroni soup, fried eggs and boiled rice, pork chops, leg of pork with whole baked plantains, pork cutlets with onions and strips of baked plantains, black beans, sweets (fruit cut in strips), and coffee and cigarettes. Eustace recorded that 'it was exceedingly kind and hospitable of the Governor, but we should have been quite satisfied with ¼ of the feast'. The next day, the brave hunters went off again in the launch and steamed up the creek where they had seen the alligator. They got stuck on a mud bank several times but managed to bag two and a half brace of web-footed plover, seven brace of parrots and an iguana. They ate the parrots for breakfast, which made 'excellent eating'. After a day of hunting they returned to camp, where Bulkeley and some others had tea ready, and they sat under a tree and ate 'al fresco'. As it was getting dark, around six o'clock, the beetles started their nightly din, 'a weird sort of noise something between a hiss and a

**The hunting party on St Luke's Island.** *Sir Anthony Cooke-Yarborough*

whirr!!' They then tried to play bridge by 'the moonbeams' misty light with our lantern dimly burning', but abandoned the idea and went to bed. They then discovered that they had been invaded by hermit crabs, which 'waddled on our bedding', but were relieved not to be attacked by mosquitoes or red ants. However, at 2.00 am they discovered that the tide was coming in, and by 3.00 am it was lapping around the tents, so at 4.30 am, they rose, had tea and biscuits and waited for the sun to rise! On Christmas Eve, Earl Fitzwilliam arrived back, having solved the problem of competing concessions, and the whole party celebrated Christmas Day 1904 on the *Véronique*.

## The explosion
On Boxing Day, they sailed for Cocos Island, 400 miles to the south. They anchored in a wooded bay on 27 December. Earl Fitzwilliam, Admiral Palliser and Frank Brooke formed a reconnaissance party, armed with the treasure map to see if they could recognise any feature described on it. But after spending half an hour slipping and sliding around, they were forced to return to the ship's boat in search of a better landing

place and somewhere to pitch the tents. With the aid of field glasses, they could all see that the land rose steeply from the sea on all sides and was almost entirely covered with dense vegetation. There was only one small piece of level sand that would be suitable for a camp site, and it took them the best part of a day, in torrential rain, to unload. They were also hampered by a large number of sharks in the waters and the need to take evasive action. Unloading the Jersey cow was an especially delicate procedure but once on land, she settled down and immediately began to devour the fresh grass. What the reconnaissance party had found was that the general area in which the map said the treasure was buried was covered by landslides, caused, they believed, by heavy tropical rains and earthquakes, and the cave entrances could not be found.

While they were setting up camp they received a visit from the island's governor, a German by the name of August Gissler. He pointed out that as far as he was aware, the sole permission to search for treasure had been given to Gray's party and they should not be there. But Earl Fitzwilliam assured the Governor that he had seen the President personally and had the government's permission to land and to search.

**The British camp with Bulkeley, Fitzwilliam and Gissler, Chatham Bay.** *Roy Young/Wentworth Garden Centre*

After several days of searching without success they decided to blast through a 300-foot high slope of scree that covered a vertical cliff face, in the hope of exposing some cave entrances. But errors were made in setting the charges. When the charge went off, a dull roar was heard and some of the material was loosened. At that point, the party of men started to make their way up the boulder-strewn slope. When they were part way up, another series of explosions, much greater than the original one, occurred and almost every one of them was at least partly buried in debris. The Earl suffered a severe head cut but others were much worse off. Bulkeley was knocked unconscious and sustained a head injury, and another had broken ribs and collar bone. The most severely wounded man had a broken leg, a broken arm and several broken ribs. One man was completely buried, and in order to rescue him they had to break the leg of another man who was wedged between two boulders on top of the buried man. After nightfall, the *Véronique* returned to the bay, and a hold on the ship was turned into an operating theatre where cuts were bandaged and broken limbs put in casts. Two days later, on 1 January 1905, they left Cocos Island, bound once again for Panama, much the worse for wear and with no sign whatsoever of the treasure. They arrived back in Panama on 3 January.

**The 'explosion' cartoon.**

The most severely wounded were left in an American hospital in Panama, while the able-bodied left the *Véronique* and were transported across the isthmus by the American authorities on a special train to the port of Colon, where on 6 January they caught the Royal Mail steamship *Orinoco* and set sail for England via Jamaica, Trinidad and Barbados. Passengers and crew lining the deck must have wondered who the bandaged group of men were as they slowly came on board. They were still carrying pots of orchids in an attempt to keep up the illusion that they had been on a scientific expedition.

## Their return

When they reached Plymouth on 26 January on their way to Southampton, they found that news and rumours about the expedition and about the explosions and injuries had preceded them. As they approached the harbour they were met by a fleet of boats carrying reporters from 'half the papers in England'. By the time they reached Southampton, they had come up with a subterfuge to keep Earl Fitzwilliam away from the press. David Smith took on the role of his valet and boarded the London express. Convinced that the Earl was also on the train, the press boarded too. The Earl stayed on the *Orinoco* until they had gone, and then disembarked without any trouble. He was met by the Countess; they breakfasted and then took the train to London to their town house in Grosvenor Square before travelling on to Wentworth Woodhouse.

That was not the end of it. National and local newspapers had a field day embroidering the story, making it up as they went along, and the Earl and his private secretary had to make statements and give interviews; it is not surprising that they were 'economical with the truth'. For example, on 28 January 1905, a report appeared in the *Rotherham Advertiser*. After wrongly describing the *Véronique* as an 'old battleship' and locating Cocos Island in the South Pacific, the long report went on to record in detail the results of an interview between the Earl and a *Daily Mail* correspondent. In the interview, the Earl rightly denied that eight members of the treasure party had been killed or that there had been a pitched battle with Mr Gray's rival treasure-hunting party. He described the effects of the explosion in great detail, saying with a grim smile that it was the narrowest escape from death that he had experienced, but he still denied that they had been looking for treasure, stating that the sole object of the expedition had been a search for minerals on the mainland of Costa Rica and on neighbouring islands, and that only a 'passing call' had been made at the so-called treasure island. He claimed that he had to be back in London for the opening of Parliament and that 'there was no time for a systematic quest of treasure, even if I had been so disposed'. This only fuelled the fire and the newspaper men continued to hound and stalk Fitzwilliam for a while before moving on to other stories, but not before publishing a less than complimentary cartoon lampooning him and suggesting that his activities might start a 'society craze' for treasure hunting.

But despite the Earl's emphatic denials there had also been diplomatic rumblings about the expedition. The Earl was summoned to Buckingham Palace for a 'wigging' from King Edward VII. The legend has it that when the interview was over, the King rose from his chair and said, 'You know perfectly well that you ought not to have done it, but – by God, I wish I had been with you.'

## British expeditions between the wars

As we know, Fitzwilliam came back empty-handed. Although it was rumoured that he planned to return to Cocos Island, he seems to have made no definite plan to do so; but others did. Indeed, there was a veritable boom in treasure hunting of all kinds in the 1920s and 1930s, both in Britain and America, and not all the adventurers were as scrupulous as the 7th Earl had been in 1904–1905.

In 1926, Sir Malcolm Campbell (1885–1948) took up the challenge. In the late 1920s he travelled to Cocos Island with Lee Guinness (1887–1937), a member of the Irish brewing family. Guinness provided the yacht, suitably called *Adventuress*, and they were able, now, to use the Panama Canal, opened in 1913. Campbell describes the wonder of this in his book, *My Greatest Adventure*.[3] Modern technology does not appear to have been of great assistance to him: after many frustrating experiments with electrical metal detectors, he concluded that these were of little use. As a result, he seems to have been reliant on having an accurate map or 'clue', showing the supposed location of a cave where the treasure was to be found.

Campbell found nothing, though he spent three times as long on the island as Fitzwilliam had done. Nevertheless, he still had faith that there was treasure awaiting discovery, despite being told that someone had once found it and taken part of it away. Indeed, in 1932 he set up a company, with the aid of a Colonel Leckie, in order to finance further attempts to find the treasure. This was Cocos Island Treasure Ltd., and the company issued a prospectus featuring a galleon on the cover, referring to Colonel Leckie's new metal detecting device – the 'Metalophone' – as a crucial tool in the company's possession, and promising investors a return of $600 for every $2 they were willing to contribute.

The expedition never even left Vancouver. The promise did, however, come to the attention of one investor who proved – at least in certain circles – to be Campbell's nemesis. This was Admiral B.M. Chambers; his trenchant critique of the search for the Treasure of Lima was published three years later.

By 1931, the phrase 'Cocos Island treasure' had entered the language, albeit temporarily. It now indicated a windfall that would rescue the indigent from money worries; but some of those who went to the Island could have done with financial assistance before they set off. Commander James Plumpton was one, since his expedition of 1932 operated on a shoestring. Plumpton had radios – both a Marconi set and an Eddystone four valve – but his small wooden sailing ship, the *Vigilant*, built by Uphams of Brixham, weighed only 50 tons, whereas Fitzwilliam's *Véronique* (for example) had been a steamship, 350 feet long, weighing 3,264 tons and capable of making over 300 miles a day. This explains why Plumpton took four months to make the voyage from England to Cocos Island, despite the opening of the Panama Canal in the meantime.

When it came to finding buried treasure, Plumpton was initially dependent on the expertise of his companion Frank Cooper, who supposedly had an uncanny ability to detect precious metal with a spring extracted from an old gramophone. Once arrived on Cocos, they fell in with a party of Canadians who were engaged in the same search as they were, and they had a Metalophone.[4]

The two parties agreed to join forces, but in the event, the Metalophone did not work. Nevertheless, Plumpton did not think that the device was entirely without merit. Undaunted by his failure, he made a second voyage and, once again, took Frank Cooper with him. The newspapers speculated that the aim was to find a sunken Spanish galleon, full of gold bullion and silver cannons, although Plumpton did not reveal their destination. However, this time our bold adventurers ran out of luck rather more quickly. Their ship, the *France,* foundered in a storm some 33 miles off Guiana. Plumpton was found, after he had drifted for four days on the wreckage, but Frank Cooper never was. His widow gave a heart-rending interview afterwards to the press, from which it was clear that Frank was a born adventurer, unable to resist the call of the sea.[5]

Gissler, Earl Fitzwilliam, Campbell and Plumpton never found anything, but they all thought that it would be worthwhile to return to Cocos Island for a second try. None of them saw through the myth to the reality, which was that there was nothing of any pecuniary value there in the first place. Some of the adventurers placed their hopes in modern science and thought that if the right equipment was deployed, this would facilitate the search. This was certainly the view taken by the Canadian company that had developed the Metalophone. They ceased trading early in 1933, but in 1934, a new company was formed.

Treasure Recovery Ltd. was floated on the Stock Exchange with the aim of raising £75,000 to finance a search for the 'numerous treasures' to be found on Cocos Island. The prospectus described the shares as 'definitely speculative', but observed that, according to the *Peace Handbook 1920*, the existence of treasure on the island was 'well established'. The promoters of the company were well-connected, and tried to exploit the strength of British snobbery. They pointed out that previous treasure hunters had included a belted earl, a knight of the realm, a senior army officer and a Royal Navy commander.

In the company's prospectus, and again upon embarkation, the chief promoter of the enterprise, Captain Arthur, claimed that he would use only the latest equipment: an aeroplane for surveying, electrical instruments for exploration, telephones for communication, and the latest drills for digging. The treasure awaiting discovery was now estimated to be worth from £12 million to £25 million, and Arthur claimed that he knew exactly where to find it. But, such was the lack of planning that he did not even bother to ask the Costa Ricans for permission to land. Instead, he laid claim to the island in the name of the British Crown, and hoisted the Union Jack upon his arrival there. Unfortunately for him, the British Government saw no reason to back his piratical adventure and it ended badly for everyone concerned.[6]

Some of Treasure Recovery's creditors asked the High Court in London to wind up the company, and their petition was granted in May 1936, leaving 1,500 creditors in the lurch. Others took action against Captain Arthur personally, and this eventually resulted in his bankruptcy. The Official Receiver informed the creditors' meeting that Arthur could not be found, because he had now gone fishing in Trinidad.[7]

The expeditions that were sent out to Cocos Island in the period between the world wars make Earl Fitzwilliam's adventure of 1904–1905 seem more like an episode from Michael Palin's *Ripping Yarns* rather than something that actually happened. The Earl's expedition was undertaken in a more innocent age, by men who may have been wanting in 'know-how', but possessed what might be called 'moral fibre' and a sense of adventure.

*Chapter 10*

# CELEBRATORY EVENTS

C elebratory events took so many forms: a dinner to mark the near completion of a building project, royal visits, christenings, birthdays, succession to a title, a golden wedding, turning of the first sod at the sinking of a colliery, sports days, hunt balls ... the list is almost endless. And many of these events were recorded on family photographs and picture postcards, in recollections of attendees, newspaper reports and, in one case, in the journal of one of the heads of the family. The large, ostentatious and costly celebrations were matched by small inexpensive ones. For example, on 9 August 1788, it is recorded in the household accounts that three shillings were paid to a Thomas Hobson 'for bread for the Masons when the top Stone of the Mausoleum was set'.[1] The Mausoleum was a cenotaph for the 2nd Marquis of Rockingham, who had died in 1782. The household accounts noted that 'Lord Milton was present'. He was of course the future 5th Earl Fitzwilliam.

**A dinner to celebrate a birthday and the near completion of the Baroque mansion**
Detailed extracts from Thomas Watson-Wentworth's (the future 1st Marquis) journal form the basis of Chapter 3. In that journal he also recorded the details of a great dinner party that he organised to mark two important events: his son Thomas's birthday (9 January 1733) and the 'Hanselling of the new offices', i.e. the coming into use of new rooms in his newly built Baroque mansion.[2] He recorded that there were about a thousand guests including not only 'Neighbouring Gentlemen' but also 'all my Tenants in the Neighbourhood'.

He describes how the food was laid out in the dining room, prayer room, old laundry, old store room and old kitchen. All the guests had tickets telling them 'which room to repair to'. Men and women were separated and they were taken to 'the best Rooms & the Inferior according to their Rank'. He then goes on to list all the dishes that were served – 225 in all. They comprised: 'of Beef 43, of Pork 30, Venison Pastys 24, Turkeys 15, Geese 21, Puddings 50, Apple or Minced Pyes 16, Fowls 14, Boar's Heads 14, Mutton 28, one hundred sixpenny loaves of White Bread, about eight Hogsheads of Ale and three of small Beer, twelve Dozen of Wine and Two Hogsheads of Punch'. One hogshead of beer was given to the poor the next day. Unfortunately, one guest died. The future 1st Marquis recorded the event in his journal as 'too melancholy a thing happened, a poor man dyed, as supposed by a Fall, in the Courtyard being in Liquor'.

**The ball to celebrate the 5th Earl's succession to the title**
The 5th Earl Fitzwilliam inherited the title in 1833 on the death of his father, the 4th Earl. But he did not celebrate his inheritance until the year after his father's death.

A celebration immediately following the death of his father would have been insensitive. But a grand ball did take place on the night of 30 September 1834. A local man, Joseph Woodcock, a brush manufacturer from Sheffield, watched the guests arriving from a viewpoint in the park and then wheedled his way into the mansion to look at the ballroom. He wrote everything up afterwards in what he called 'Remarks of passing events', which he said were 'homely but warranted faithful'.[3]

Woodcock noted that from the park in front of the Palladian mansion, at about eight o'clock when they arrived, they could see that the servants were lighting the ballroom where the ball was going to be held. This was in fact the Marble Saloon. At about ten minutes past nine, the first carriages started to arrive. At first they 'parked in a single line in front of the mansion but this soon became a double line, then a treble line and finally a quadruple line'. It was not until after eleven o'clock that the last carriage arrived, by which time they were parked for 2 miles across the park in the direction of Greasbrough. He reckoned that altogether there were about 700 carriages, mostly each pulled by two horses, but with some pulled by four horses. By the time the last carriages arrived he said there were also thousands of spectators outside the mansion.

Having seen during the evening through the downstairs windows of the right-hand side of the mansion the cooks assembling food, he was keen to get inside. He was joined by two male friends and his cousin Anne, and she managed to persuade someone to let the small party inside through the doorway leading to the servants' hall. They then went along a passage and up the stairs, and looked through the half-open door into the Marble Saloon. Woodcock said that the Marble Saloon was lit with 'upwards of five thousand oil lamps, some of them variegated, but chiefly without colour'. They were arranged in rows beneath the balustrades of the gallery that circles the room halfway between the floor and the ceiling. He also said that there were lights in other parts of the room, including lamps and candles hanging from the chandelier that was suspended from the ceiling in the middle of the room. The effect of all the lamps and candles was to make the room 'one blaze of light' and gave 'the most extraordinary charm to the rich dresses of the ladies'. It was, he said, 'the most magnificent coup d'oeil I ever beheld', which was 'almost too grand for description'. They then managed to sneak up into the gallery to look down on the ballroom below. From there something else caught Woodcock's attention: the statues in the alcoves around the walls of the Marble Saloon that had been bought by the 2nd Marquis of Rockingham in Italy while on his Grand Tour nearly a century earlier. Woodcock said they were 'shockingly indecent and a great reflection upon the taste of the noble proprietor and do not say much in favour of the modesty of the higher classes'.

The music for the dances was provided by a famous London band, Weppert's Royal Quadrille Band, which was well regarded by Queen Victoria and Prince Albert. Woodcock said, 'the dancing consisted entirely of quadrilles and gallopades'. The gallopade was a relatively new dance introduced into England from the Continent in 1829. The ball was 'led off by the Duke of Devonshire and the hon. Miss Wentworth'.

As they left the mansion they saw the supper tables laid out with food for the guests. These included beef in the shape of a soldier's helmet, a boar's head with its ears and nose tipped with gold, and a selection of other savoury dishes that he could not recognise, including shellfish three times the size of shrimps. Before they left at about four o'clock in the morning, they were allowed to sit on a form at a table in the servants' hall and have a light meal consisting of a saddle of mutton and bread with a glass of 'stingo' (a strong ale aged in oak casks).

## The golden wedding of the 6th Earl and Countess Fitzwilliam in 1888

The 6th Earl married Lady Harriet Douglas on 10 September 1838. And fifty years later, in September 1888, they celebrated their golden wedding. The celebrations at Wentworth went on for twelve days. They began on 8 September with a tea party in the park for 4,000 children who attended schools on the estate. This was followed, on 10 September, the day itself, by a procession from the mansion along Main Street to the Trinity church beneath a succession of triumphal arches, carrying the Fitzwilliams' and the Countess's family mottoes: *Appetitus Rationi Pareat* (Let your desire be governed by reason) and *Lock Sicker* (Be sure). At the church a thanksgiving service was held and the church bells rang all day. In the evening, the Earl and Countess were 'at home' to friends and tenants. On 15 September, the miners from the Earl's collieries and their wives were entertained to tea accompanied by a fireworks display, Morris dancing, maypole dancing and a torchlight procession around the mansion. Two days later, on 17 September, the children from the infant schools and pre-school children were invited to another tea party, and on 18 September, members of various churches' mothers' groups were also entertained to tea. Finally, on 19 September, estate employees had a dinner followed by a ball in the Marble Saloon. A local

**A drawing of the 6th Earl & Countess Fitzwilliam.** *Illustrated London News, 1888*

composer, Tom Nock from Hoyland, who was blind, composed a polka, the *Wentworth Woodhouse Polka*. It was dedicated to the Countess and was danced at the ball. Other presents were an oak cross presented by the estate's coal miners, a portrait of the Countess by Hubert von Herkomer and another painting of the family at a meeting of the Wentworth hunt.

The golden wedding received national publicity. The *Illustrated London News* did a seven-page special feature about Wentworth Woodhouse on 8 September.[4] The writer said that Wentworth Park would be the venue of 'the greatest festival it has ever known'. The feature included twenty line drawings of the Earl and Countess, the house, exterior and interior, and the park (four of which showed deer grazing).

### Visit of the Prince and Princess of Wales in 1891 to open Clifton Park, Rotherham

The official opening of Clifton Park took place on 25 June 1891 and was conducted by the Prince and Princess of Wales (later King Edward VII and Queen Alexandra) accompanied by Princesses Maud and Victoria. The opening was a splendid royal and, it must be said, hilarious occasion in part. The royal party spent the previous night at Wentworth Woodhouse in the company of the 6th Earl and Countess Fitzwilliam. At the opening ceremony, as the leading local figure, was the mayor of Rotherham, Alderman Neill, bedecked in his newly acquired cocked hat and mayoral chain of office (made by local jeweller John Mason). The mayor must have looked particularly regal to the local juvenile population because when he and his wife arrived at the park ahead of the royal party and stepped down from their carriage, 10,000 children on specially erected stands mistook him for the royal personage and began to sing their well-rehearsed song, *God Bless the Prince of Wales*, to 'considerable merriment', as the *Rotherham Advertiser* put it.[5] Clifton Park was duly declared open by the Prince of Wales, who was then presented with a silver gilt casket specially designed by Alderman Mason. After the opening ceremony the royal party was accompanied to Clifton House for lunch. Clifton House became Clifton Park Museum in 1893.

During the afternoon and evening of the opening day there was an exciting programme of events for the large crowds to enjoy including bands playing, dancing and a firework display. But the main attraction was a balloon ascent by a Captain Whelan of Huddersfield. At the beginning of the ascent there was a near calamity when a local councillor got his legs entangled with the ropes and was almost carried aloft hanging upside down. Fortunately, he just managed to free himself before the balloon ascended and drifted upwards to land on the moors several miles to the west.

### The christening of Peter, the future 8th Earl Fitzwilliam, in 1911

The christening of Peter, Viscount Milton, at Wentworth Woodhouse in 1911 was a major celebration, not just for the family but for many thousands of their friends, tenants and the local population in general. The whole event was captured on a series of postcards by E.L. Scrivens, the Doncaster-based photographer. They included a nurse showing off the baby to photographers, cups and bowls being presented to the Earl and Countess, the roasting of an ox for sandwiches, and the firework display that accompanied the christening.

SHOWING THE BABY
VISCOUNT MILTON

**Peter, Viscount Milton, on his christening day, 1911.** *Bill Dunigan*

The event was more like a coronation than a christening. This was because the 7th Earl and Countess had had four daughters (Elfrida, Donatia, Joan and Helena); daughters could not inherit a title and it was feared that the earldom would go to another branch of the family. The relative who would inherit if there was no son was an uncle, the Hon. William Henry Fitzwilliam, who was 70 years old. The christening, therefore, was not just the celebration of a new life but a relief that the earldom would stay in the immediate family. Peter became 8th Earl in 1943, but was killed in an aircraft accident in 1948.

The christening ceremony took place in the mansion's private chapel at one o'clock on Saturday, 12 February 1911. The service was conducted by the Reverend R.E.W. Verini, vicar of Wentworth and the Earl's private chaplain. The *Rotherham Advertiser* reported that the scarf presented to the Earl's ancestor at the Battle of Hastings for his 'valour and service' would be wrapped around the baby Peter.[6] This was a longstanding Fitzwilliam tradition. The ceremony was attended by just the family and relatives. Viscount Milton was christened William Henry Laurence Peter. The godfathers were the Hon. William Henry Fitzwilliam and the Marquis of Zetland (father of Countess Fitzwilliam), and the godmother was the Duchess of Buccleuch.

Seven thousand invitations were sent out to official guests, and in addition, the grounds at the mansion were thrown open to the public. It was reported that 50,000 to

100,000 of the general public were expected to turn up. The *Rotherham Advertiser* did not think that the estimate was an extravagant one. This was because the Earl was not only an important landlord but a very significant employer, and his influence, directly and indirectly on people's lives for many miles around, was immense.

The 1,000 official guests dined in the riding school in the stable block and in six enormous marquees. One hundred men from London were sent to erect marquees and 300 waiters were sent by the caterers, Lyons of London, to Wentworth by special train. Lyons also supplied 17,000 sandwiches, 10,000 meat pies, 30,000 cakes and buns, 2,000 gallons of beer, and poured thousands of cups of tea. The general public were given the opportunity to buy beef sandwiches, the beef being cut from a roasted ox.

After the christening ceremony at about two o'clock, a series of presentations took place on the steps in front of the mansion. Local tenants, the employees of the hunts that the Earl rode to hounds with, the parishioners of Wentworth and local miners all presented engraved bowls. A two-handled inscribed silver bowl was presented to the Earl and Countess for the infant heir by the Earl's tenants of Greasbrough, Rawmarsh,

**The amazing fireworks display at the christening.** *Bill Dunigan*

Upper Haugh, Thorpe Hesley and Scholes. Another was presented by the employees of the four local foxhunts with which the Earl was closely associated (Wentworth, Cantley, Yacht and Grove), and a third, an antique porringer, by the parishioners of Wentworth. A fourth silver bowl, presented by the miners of Elsecar Main and Low Stubbin collieries, was used at the christening itself. To coincide with the birth of a male heir, Whitworth, Son & Nephew of Wath upon Dearne made a special brew of ale that was delivered to be stored in the vaults at Wentworth Woodhouse. It was intended that these 'tremendous number of hogsheads', to quote the *Rotherham Advertiser*, would sit for twenty-one years and then be consumed on the Viscount's coming of age in 1931.[7]

In the afternoon and evening there was a full round of festivities including bands, roundabouts and daylight fireworks. The event ended with a magnificent fireworks display, which started at a quarter to six, when it was quite dark. Managed by the firm of Brocks, it was reputed to be the biggest private fireworks display for five years. It included portraits of the Earl and Countess with the motto 'Long Live the Heir', Niagara Falls rolling its waters down 'in limpid fire', and a British battleship attacking and sinking the 'dreadnought' of a continental power.

### The visit of King George V and Queen Mary in 1912

This was part of the King's 'Tour of the North', i.e. the West Riding of Yorkshire, at the suggestion of the Archbishop of York, Cosmo Gordon Lang, who was a personal friend of and close advisor to the King. This was a period of industrial unrest and strikes, and of trades union upheaval. In 1911 there had been a national dock strike and a national railway strike, and in March 1912, one million miners went on strike. Those in power feared a general strike. A visit from the King and Queen, in essence, a public relations exercise, was hoped to provide a calming influence. As the *Rotherham Advertiser* put it, the visit had been arranged so that Their Majesties could see 'different classes of toilers at work'. The newspaper went on to say that they would witness:

> many phases of industrial life. They will see the ironworker at the furnace, the miner plying his pick and shovel at the coal face, and the weavers of worsted and woollen earning their livelihoods amidst the whirr and burr of thousands of looms.[8]

The King and Queen wanted no fuss, no fanfare, no expensive decorations on the routes that they would travel on; but as the *Rotherham Advertiser* pointed out, this would not prevent tradesmen and others displaying flags and bunting from their premises, and for crowds of people to line the routes – which they did in large numbers.

The visit began on Monday, 8 July 1912 and ended on Friday morning, 12 July. The programme was very full. From Monday to Thursday, they visited the Lord Mayor of Rotherham at Clifton Park (which the King's father, Edward, the Prince of Wales, had opened in 1891); Conisbrough Castle, near the pit village of Denaby Main; Cadeby Main Colliery, where there were two horrific explosions on 9 July in which eighty-eight men lost their lives; Silverwood Colliery at Thrybergh; Woodlands 'model' village, next to Brodsworth Main Colliery, near Doncaster, where they visited one of the new miners'

F. P. S. The King At Elsecar Colliery, July 9 1912.

**King George V visiting Elsecar Colliery in 1912.**

houses and were given a tour by the owners, William and Sarah Brown; Hickleton Hall, where they dined with the owner, Lord Halifax; and Elsecar Main Colliery, where the King descended the shaft to view working conditions. Everywhere they went the crowds were immense and brass bands played the national anthem. Their visit to Cadeby Main Colliery was a very sad occasion and Queen Mary was seen in tears.

During their five-day tour of the mining districts of South Yorkshire they stayed with the 7th Earl Fitzwilliam and Countess Maud at Wentworth Woodhouse, where they were greeted on their arrival by a large crowd, estimated at 40,000, filling the park in front of the mansion. The evenings were full because during their stay at Wentworth Woodhouse, the Earl and Countess had also invited a house party of more than thirty of the great and the good, including the King's private secretary, two equerries, the Archbishop of York, a dozen titled gentlemen and their wives, and relatives of the Earl and Countess. And, of course, these house guests were accompanied by a retinue of servants. The dinners on the Monday, Tuesday and Wednesday evenings were grand affairs. The visit of the reigning king and queen may have had a political rather than a purely social purpose, but for the Earl and Countess it celebrated their local, regional and national standing.[9]

**Fox hunts, hunt balls and other sporting events**
Foxhunting was banned by law in England and Wales in 2005 and in Scotland three years earlier, in 2002. But for centuries, it was an integral part of life on the country estates of the rich and titled. The hunting season lasted from November until March.

The activity was not just restricted to the aristocracy and the upper classes. Writing in *Blackwood's Magazine* in 1934, David Smith, son of Francis Patrick Smith of Barnes Hall, in Ecclesfield, painted a vivid picture of the Boxing Day hunt at Wentworth in the early years of the twentieth century. Before the hunt got on its way, he said, 'a drink of cherry brandy sets their circulation going'. But he went on to state that the Boxing Day hunt at Wentworth was a 'foot people's festival'. He said people 'come in their hundreds from the surrounding villages and track after the hounds … with unbounded enthusiasm'.[10]

On the Wentworth estate, the fox hunts roamed far and wide in the surrounding area. Take, for example, the hunt that took place on Monday, 24 November 1913. The hunt met at Thundercliffe Grange, just over 2 miles south of Wentworth Woodhouse, the home of Dr and Mrs Mould. Participants included the Countess Fitzwilliam and her four daughters, Ladies Elfrida, Joan, Donatia and Helena, and Viscount Carlton (later Earl of Wharncliffe), who married Lady Elfrida in 1918. On a beautiful sunny morning, according to the report in the *Rotherham Advertiser*,[11] the first unsuccessful draw was in Woolley Wood, at that time belonging to the Duke of Norfolk. The pack then returned to Grange Park at Thundercliffe and went through Barber Wood, Walkworth Wood and Gallery Bottom, again drawing a blank. A fox was chased up Grange Lane towards Thorpe Hesley village. It was then followed through Scholes Coppice and into the park at Wentworth, where it was lost. A second fox was hunted in Mausoleum Wood but it went to ground in a rabbit burrow near Upper Haugh, and another took refuge in a backyard at Greasbrough. The final draw was in Trowles Wood and Temple Wood in the park. It came to an end at four o'clock.

One minor celebratory hunt event also took place in 1913. This was Peter, the future 8th Earl's, first meet – well, not quite. Local photographer E.L. Scrivens, who had produced a whole range of postcards of his christening, was on hand to record the event. On the postcard Peter sits proudly on his horse. In fact, he was frightened of horses in his infancy and after the photograph was taken, he was carried away by his nurse and spent the rest of the morning in the nursery!

Fox hunts were accompanied by point-to-point horse races, house parties and an annual hunt ball. The hunt ball started off with cocktails, followed by dinner and then dancing. In the mid- and late-1940s until his death in 1948, Peter, then the 8th Earl, spent much time on the Coollattin estate in Ireland, where fox hunts and point-to-point races were very much part of the sporting scene. In 1945 or 1946, one estate worker, Paddy Behan, recalled that the first hunt ball at that time was held in the Courthouse in Shillelagh, close to Coollattin House.[12] A Dublin firm of caterers was hired to provide the food and a popular band, Peggy Dell and her Orchestra, provided the music. At the end of the evening it was the custom to sing the national anthem, and *God Save the King* was played. What must be remembered is that Irish independence had been won and recognised in 1922. It was a foreign country, to all intents and purposes. Apparently, some of those present were Republicans and one went on stage and kicked his foot through the big drum. After that the hunt ball was held at Coollattin House.

There is an interesting story connected with one of the annual sports days at Wentworth Woodhouse. It is said that Lady Mabel, the 7th Earl's sister (1870–1951), as a young teenager was a very good sprinter and she had only one other close rival. One year she turned up to the sports day to find that her rival was not there. On enquiring about where she was, she was told that the girl had reached the age of 13, had left school and had to leave the area to work in service as a domestic servant. This had a profound effect on Lady Mabel. She spent a large part of her adult life campaigning for better educational opportunities for young people, especially girls. She was a member of the West Riding Education Committee, was a member of the Labour Party, and was instrumental in the founding of Ecclesfield Grammar School. From 1949 to 1976, Wentworth Woodhouse was the home of the Label Mabel College, a physical education teachers' training college.

*Chapter 11*

# SOME MILITARY USES OF WENTWORTH WOODHOUSE

## Lords Lieutenant of the West Riding of Yorkshire

Lieutenants for various counties were first appointed by Henry VIII in the 1540s, when England stood in danger of foreign invasion. They took over responsibility for the local militia from the medieval sheriffs, a responsibility that was not removed until 1871, though they could still call upon able-bodied men to fight when needed, as late as 1921. In the eighteenth century, the 1st and 2nd Marquises of Rockingham were Lords Lieutenant of the West Riding of Yorkshire, while in the nineteenth century, the 4th and 6th Earls Fitzwilliam held that office. At all relevant times, these Lieutenants had their principal seat at Wentworth Woodhouse.

The importance of the post in the eighteenth century is exemplified in a notice that appeared in the *Leeds Intelligencer* on Tuesday, 9 March 1756 – the year that saw the outbreak of the Seven Years' War of 1756–63:

1 March, 1756.

WHEREAS General Napier's Regiment of foot is ordered into the West Riding of the County of York, to recruit the same; and will be at LEEDS (their Head Quarters) on or about Wednesday se'night[1] and several Recruiting Officers will be sent to most of the principal Towns in the said County.

These are to inform such Persons who not did choose to enlist for Life that in the said Regiment they may do it for three Years, or during the Continuance of the War: And that to Men 5 Foot 8 Inches high, or upwards, in their Shoes, there will be given by the recruiting Officers at the Time of their enlisting, the Sum of Two Guineas, and Half a Guinea more when they shall join the Regiment. To Men from five Foot five Inches without their Shoes, to five Foot eight Inches with their Shoes, will be given a Guinea and Half, and Half a Guinea more when they come to the Regiment. And as a further Encouragement the Marquis of Rockingham proposes to give One Guinea to every Yorkshire Man (over and above what will be given by the recruiting Officers) who shall enlist into the said Regiment within the Space of one Month from the Date hereof, to be paid at Wentworth House, or by GEORGE THOMPSON, Esq. at York; JAMES PRESTON, Esq. at Malton; or by Lieutenant-Colonel Buck, of the said Regiment, to be quarter'd at Leeds; or by JEREMIAH DIXON, of the same Place.

And that the Persons who shall enter into the Service in Consequence of this Encouragement may be the better known, his Lordship has ordered a List of them to be kept that they may meet with the Favour they shall deserve on their Discharge from the Service, at their Return home.

NB A proper Person will attend at Wentworth-House every Tuesday and Thursday for the space of one Mouth, to receive such Persons as shall be able and willing to enlist into the said Regiment.

The Seven Years' War was highly successful from the British point of view: it saw the famous 'Year of Victories' in 1759 and meant that the French were no longer a rival to Britain in Canada and India. However, it was followed by the disastrous American War of Independence, from 1776 to 1783, which led to the formation of the United States and the loss of 'the First British Empire'. The 2nd Marquis of Rockingham was a leading politician and opposed the war, taking the view that the Americans should be allowed, by and large, to govern themselves. Nevertheless, he played a prominent role in organising the defence of Hull against the privateer John Paul Jones, and subsidised the Wicklow Volunteers (since his family had enormous estates in Ireland).[2]

The 4th Earl Fitzwilliam was Lord Lieutenant from 1798 to 1819, and therefore held that office for much of the French Revolutionary and Napoleonic Wars – a period when large numbers of local men served in the armed forces. There is no space here to relate the vigorous but sometimes amusing efforts of the Rotherham Volunteers to resist invasion by the French Emperor, but they were fully chronicled by John Guest in his monumental *Historic Notices of Rotherham* (1879).

Sheffield gained an early reputation as a hotbed of civil unrest and even sedition. In August 1812, it was reported that conspirators in the town were planning to march on Wentworth Woodhouse, while in October, a government informant related how he had met a group of men in an alehouse who thought that 'everything is wrong in this country, from King to the Constable, and Bonaparte is an honest fellow'. In June 1817 (after Napoleon had been finally sent into exile), Sheffield magistrates even discovered a plan by home-grown revolutionaries to storm Wentworth Woodhouse, as well as the Sheffield barracks and the arms depot at Doncaster. Troops were also sent to guard Wentworth Woodhouse during the coal riots of 1893, something that should be borne in mind when we talk about the long period of peace enjoyed by this country under Queen Victoria.[3]

Yet it is noteworthy that the 4th Earl was a Whig, at a time when the Tories almost monopolised the government of Britain; he even earned a reputation for being something of a Liberal, in that he favoured Catholic Emancipation and resigned his office of

**Local militia.** *Eric Leslie*

Lord Lieutenant of Ireland in 1795 on this issue. Likewise, he was dismissed from his office of Lord Lieutenant of the West Riding in 1819, after he had protested against the use of excessive violence by the authorities at the so-called Peterloo massacre in Manchester.

The late 1850s and 1860s were a time of renewed Anglo-French hostility and there were serious fears that the Emperor Napoleon III of France might attempt an invasion of these islands. This was what led to the building or reinforcement of many of the Martello towers on the south coast. It also led to the formation in 1859 of the Volunteer Force, a citizen army that later merged with the Territorial Army. In 1867, the *Sheffield Independent* for Tuesday, 5 November carried the following report:

> Last evening, the Countess Fitzwilliam presented a number of money and other prizes which have been won by members of our Artillery corps during this and the previous year ... The members of the No. 1 Battery formed a guard of honour, and were stationed at the entrance to the hall and on the staircase. Each side of the hall was occupied by members of other batteries, and as the Countess Fitzwilliam was led on to the platform by Lieut. Colonel Creswick, these gave a military salute. Earl FITZWILLIAM said: I thank you on Lady Fitzwilliam's behalf for the opportunity you have given her of coming among you, and presenting to each successful man the various prizes which by your skill you have won.

When the Territorial Army was formed by Lord Haldane in 1908, because of mounting concern about the military power and intentions of Imperial Germany, most towns in the country raised units as second-line battalions of the local infantry regiment, but great landowners tended to sponsor mounted units. So it was that the 7th Earl Fitzwilliam raised a battery of Royal Horse Artillery at Wentworth, though he was an officer in the Oxfordshire Light Infantry. Only £205 was made available to him to buy mounts, but he supplemented these with his own hunters, and had little trouble in recruiting men for the unit. Roy Young described how the battery went into camp in 1909 on the Handkerchief Piece in Wentworth Park, with 200 men, over 100 horses and four 15-pounder field guns.[4]

### The First World War

The Territorial Army was established for home defence but, when war with Germany broke out in August 1914, the great need was to bolster the French resistance, and so individuals were asked to volunteer for overseas service, and many did. According to Roy Young, it was said 'that none of those who did so – and who survived the horrors of the war – ever lacked employment either on the estate or in its collieries again, however much unemployment there was'.[5] In time, however, the need for more and more men became apparent, and men from the Wentworth Battery found themselves in the Middle East, while a second battery raised in 1914 also saw active service on

**A memorial in Wentworth parish church to local men of the Royal Horse Artillery who lost their lives in the First World War.**

the Western Front. There is a memorial in Wentworth parish church to eighteen local men who died serving with the Royal Horse Artillery in the First World War. Some were estate workers. Eight were buried in Egypt, five in Syria, two in Lebanon, one in Jerusalem, one in Iraq and one in Darton.

A newspaper report in the *Sheffield Evening Telegraph* gives details of an exercise carried out by Earl Fitzwilliam to test the ability of the new battery to convey field guns over a long distance:

> The battery at Wentworth Woodhouse is armed with 13-pounder guns, which were the first issued to the Territorial Horse batteries after the Force was constituted. Keen interest was felt in the operations by the military authorities, and a special report will be made to the War Office.
>
> The motors were driven by civilian drivers, and left Sheffield after midnight Friday for the gun park at Wentworth Woodhouse, where they were to pick up the guns.
>
> The scene in front of Wentworth Woodhouse, between one and two in the morning, when all was ready to start, was very picturesque. The Adjutant of the West Riding Artillery gave the novel command, 'Start your engines.' The great advantage of using a motor of the

self-starting type was noticeable as the drivers had not quit their seats. To show what was expected of the battery the roadway in front of the house was circled several times at varying speeds. Everyone who had any knowledge of the artillery arm was doubtful as to whether the wheels and carriages would stand the strain. Lord Fitzwilliam, his Adjutant, and officers were however, perfectly confident, and it may be said at once that their faith was justified.

The argument which governed the operation was set forth as follows:—For the purpose of this experiment it is assumed that war is declared by a nation 'E' inhabiting land, across the North Sea on July 17. A raiding force in transports, strongly escorted by cruisers and destroyers, is reported 35 miles east of Great Grimsby. The force is estimated at 5,000 men in two transports of 5,000 tons each. From information received the objective of enemy's raiding force is Great Grimsby. On Friday evening, July 17, a telegram is received by the officer commanding the West Riding Royal Horse Artillery at Wentworth from the General Officer Commanding in Chief, Northern command, instructing him to proceed with utmost dispatch with battery to Waltham, three miles south of Great Grimsby, and await orders there.

The railway bridges have been destroyed; the service being a most urgent one, and the distance being too great for horse traction the experiment now being carried out is to demonstrate the adaptability of motor traction for the purpose.

The journey before the battery could reach its objective was a long one, and it was complicated by the fact that the ammunition waggons had to start two hours before the guns to collect the mobilisation ammunition which was supposed to be stored in Selby at an ordnance depot.

The whole unit was to be formed up at Gainsborough complete for action, and this involved a journey for the ammunition waggons of approximately 119 miles, while the distance for the guns was practically 80.

The waggons started at two o'clock for Selby, where they waited a sufficient time to take up their load, and they then proceeded to Gainsborough to join the battery itself. There were no delays, and at half-past eleven in the morning the battery had arrived at Waltham, where, according to the 'special idea' it was to await orders.

Lieutenant-General Sir Herbert Plumer motored from his headquarters at York and accompanied the battery, observing closely throughout.

The guns reached Waltham in three hours and forty minutes from the start, their highest speed being a little over 30 miles per hour, while occasionally they dropped between 17 and 18 miles per hour.

The behaviour of the wheels, gun carriages, and waggons was surprisingly good.[6]

**A military parade marching through Wentworth village in 1914.**

**The 7th Earl Fitzwilliam in his uniform at the time of the First World War.** *David Allott/ Wentworth Woodhouse Preservation Trust*

## The Second World War

During the Second World War, parts of Wentworth Woodhouse were used by the Military Intelligence Corps, and their time there is recorded in a remarkable film, a history and two memoirs. The film, which was made in 1944, can be viewed online.[7] It deals with the motorcycle training course that the Army ran at Wentworth Woodhouse, based in the stable block, which lasted three weeks, and aimed to teach recruits not only how to ride a motorbike, but how to maintain one, and eventually how to go 'rough riding' over an obstacle course. New recruits are shown arriving at a local railway station and making their first clumsy attempts to ride their machines (some of them have great difficulty in even starting them). Then they venture out on the roads, to Hoober, to a village on the moors near Bolsterstone, and to Barnsley. Some of them take a tumble, more than once, into a hedge, but none seems the worse for wear. They ride around Wentworth Park and are shown what to do if a machine stalls while they are going uphill. (The solution is to put the machine on its side on the ground, grapple with it so that it is pointing downhill, pick it up, mount it, and kick-start it so as to go downhill, before attempting to ride back up again.) By the time the film finishes, they have mastered their machines, and they 'pass out', in the military sense.

The history and the memoirs are of broader interest because they narrate the entire history of the Military Intelligence Corps at Wentworth Woodhouse, from 1942 through to 1946, four years when it evidently played a vital role in the war effort, and when training of many types other than motorcycling was given. At the same time, these three works are very different from each other.

The history, published in 2013, is by a well-known military historian, Nick van der Bijl.[8] The passages about Wentworth tell how Wentworth Woodhouse was chosen as headquarters of the Intelligence Corps because this was expanded, especially after the USA entered the war as a result of the Japanese attack on Pearl Harbor in December 1941. In particular, the Depot, Quartermaster and Other Ranks' Wing moved into the stable block in late October 1942, while the HQ and Officers' Wing moved into the main house six months later. The cookhouse and NAAFI were located in the riding school. As for the men, they were accommodated in Nissen huts situated opposite the stable block, where the now dilapidated student residential blocks still stand.

The motorcycle course is also described. The writer tells us that it began almost as soon as the rookies arrived:

> After tea, the platoon was issued with leather motor-cycling coats, helmets and gauntlets from the Company Quartermaster and the next day they were allocated their motor-cycles from a mix of about 120 machines that included BSA 500ccs, Norton 16s, Ariel 350ccs, 350cc Royal Enfields and Matchless GL3s from several sheds.[9]

We are told how participants learned to ride on a cinder track, on roads and across country, 'negotiating obstacles from climbing slag heaps to streams'. The last two days were spent on tests, but the platoon then had a second three weeks, learning about the organisation and administration of the British Army, and doing weapons training, drill, report writing and map reading. This was followed by three weeks of exercises on the Yorkshire moors, and a final two weeks of intensive training on Field Security (at first done at Matlock, but also at Frensham, Surrey). Also, 'some students spent a week with the Sheffield City Police Criminal Investigation Department learning investigation and the application of forensic evidence.'

The training schedule at Wentworth was usually 8.45 am to 6.30 pm, Monday to Saturday, but, although conditions were described by a Canadian trainee as Spartan, van der Bijl relates that the courses were 'generally considered to be great fun' and 'recreation was not forgotten, with lorries taking off-duty soldiers to Rotherham and Sheffield either for a night out or a weekend's leave'. He also tells us that the living quarters eventually occupied by the trainee motorcyclists, which were in the stable block and were each named after a famous British battle, were quite 'luxurious', with single beds and hot and cold water.

The first memoir is that of a Frenchman, Maurice Vila, who managed to escape from France and later wrote about his experiences in Britain, in *My War in Two Armies*, published by the BBC in 2005 as part of an archive of Second World War memories.[10] The relevant section relates to the preparations for D-Day in 1943. Vila tells us that he joined the British Army in February 1943, becoming Private Vila No. 14549494 of No. 9 Squad, No. 2 Coy, No. 10 Primary Training Centre; that he underwent military training at Chichester and then applied to join the Intelligence Corps, because he thought his knowledge of languages would be of use there. His application was accepted and he soon found himself at Wentworth Woodhouse, in No. 2 Company. He describes the training he received there as more intensive and strenuous than anything he had done before, and tells us that it included a three-week course at Smedley's Hydro at Matlock, where we attended lectures 'on all aspects of security'. He also confirms that his training included the motorcycle course 'as these machines were to be our normal method of transport'. He completed his training in Yorkshire in October 1943, and was then posted to Fort William in Scotland, with the rank of lance corporal in the Intelligence Corps.[11]

The second memoir is by Llewellyn C. Fletcher, a Canadian Intelligence Corps officer, published in 2014.[12] It is interesting that Fletcher tells us that he received very little training at all at Wentworth Woodhouse. But this is doubtless explained by the fact that Fletcher's military service was undertaken after the end of the war in Europe, and indeed after the end of the war with Japan. On the other hand, he does mention the notorious open-cast mining conducted in the gardens of Wentworth Woodhouse, on the orders of 'Manny' Shinwell, and he gives us a foreigner's view of Yorkshire as a whole. He describes Wentworth Woodhouse as a 'palace' and states (incorrectly) that the frontage of 600 feet is 'exceeded only by that of Buckingham Palace'. He says (wrongly, again) that the present buildings were 'only' 300 years old, whereas in his day they were only about 200 years old, but he correctly describes the importance of Sir Thomas Wentworth, 1st Earl of Stafford. He enthuses over a tour of the house, where he saw what he considered to be, or was told, was 'the greatest in European architecture, sculpture, art, and the trophies of hunting and armour', and he was amazed by the 'orchards, herds of deer, mausoleum and cupolas' in the grounds and gardens, which for him demonstrated 'the Age of Elegance of the British aristocracy'. And he was particularly impressed when he wandered through the gardens now attached to Wentworth Garden Centre, when he came across a place where there was an inscription over a doorway:

> There is healing in a garden,
> When one longs for peace and pardon;
> Once past the gate, no need to wait,
> For God is in the garden.

Today's patrons of the garden centre can see this inscription over the entrance of the gateway to the Japanese and Italian gardens. The Canadian trainee mistook the bear pit there for a 'mysterious medieval dungeon'.

Finally, Captain Fletcher could not resist making some reflections on the changes that the wartime and post-war Labour government had brought about in British society, and also commented on the British climate. As to the former, he gave vent to a predictably colonial egalitarianism:

> Some of the nobility have been taxed out of existence or have become tourist guides in the proud houses of their ancestors, but now government-owned museums. So today they belong to the masses. It was a long time before some of us discovered that the present Earl was a modest British colonel of high caliber [*sic*] and shared our lot, undistinguished from any other officers.[13]

As to the climate, Fletcher complained that he had never suffered so much from the cold, despite being from Canada. When asked why he felt it so keenly, he replied that the British, who were so progressive in other respects, had never learned to heat their buildings properly, at least not to North American standards, and quipped that 'in our country fire is something to keep us warm, not just to look at in a fireplace'. He also remarked that the officers were little better off than the men in this respect.

> Other Ranks were unable to secure enough coal to warm the Quonset huts,[14] except at the start of day. Even officers, who occupied single rooms in the palace, each with its own fireplace, could not secure enough coal for warmth for any length of time. A few of the more corpulent British officers shut off the heat from the fireplace, first by facing it to warm their fronts, then by turning round to warm their behinds.[15]

Finally, those of us old enough to remember the old Izal toilet paper will sympathise with this *cri de coeur*:

> We had few other dislikes besides lack of heat. However, one perhaps is worth mentioning, the antiquated toilet facilities and the toilet paper, which was but a slight improvement over sandpaper.[16]

### The Military Intelligence Corps 'At Home'

On 27 July 1946, the corps staged an 'At Home' in Wentworth Park, which featured a mock battle and was reported in the *Yorkshire Post* for Monday, 29 July as follows:

> Between the elegant Georgian mansion and parkland scarred by open coal seams, gunners went into action at Wentworth Woodhouse on Saturday. South Yorkshire crowds enjoyed the smoke and explosions of this mimic battle staged by the Royal Artillery as part of an 'At Home' at the Depot of the Intelligence Corps, which is on Earl Fitzwilliam's estate. Armoured cars were spotted in a wood near the miners' excavators. Crews manning 25-pounders engaged the 'enemy' with enthusiasm. Although the ammunition was blank, it lacked nothing in noise and spectators lining the 'battlefield' were thrilled. Young visitors handled German anti-tank rifles with insatiable curiosity and broadcast to each other across the lawns on British 'walkie-talkie' sets.

In addition to this 'realistic display of guns and armour' there was a display of German maps captured by First Corps troops who had been stationed near Doncaster before D-Day. Some details of this exhibition – of material that had clearly been collected for the benefit of the German High Command but had ultimately been passed to British Intelligence – were given in a report that appeared in the *Yorkshire Post*, also for 29 July 1946:

> At the Army's 'At Home' at Wentworth Woodhouse on Saturday a fascinating sideshow was the Intelligence Corps' display of captured German documents. With keen curiosity and a sense of relief, Yorkshire visitors examined an invasion map showing Spurn Point, Cleethorpes and other well-known East Coast places as potential landing points.
>
> Books issued to German bomber crews were seen, with pictures of important targets in the North. Among such vulnerable points I noticed views of Kirkstall power station, Leeds, in an artistic setting of trees. Other places selected by the Germans for the special attention of their bomb-aimers were the ICI works at Billingham, the United Bus Company's garage at Darlington, the Staithes viaduct, a railway bridge at Northallerton, and Whiteley's cable works at Poole-in-Wharfedale.

But, intriguing though these items were, there was another that would have been of even more interest to many who attended the 'At Home' at Wentworth Woodhouse that day. This was an aerial photograph of the extensive Newton Chambers Works at Thorncliffe in Chapeltown, only a mile or so as the bomber flies from Wentworth. This northern powerhouse was a place where 1,160 Churchill tanks were manufactured. The photograph could therefore have been an invaluable source of information for German intelligence. It was taken in November 1942, before the conclusion of the Battle of

**The 1,000th Churchill tank to come off the production line at Newton Chambers.**
*Peter Leask*

Stalingrad, and therefore when Britain's fate still hung in the balance. There is a further twist to this story. Around forty years ago, when a copy of this photograph hung on the wall of a local pub, customers were told by the landlord that it demonstrated the existence of a British spy, who must have passed details to the Germans of the identification of the various buildings and installations revealed by their reconnaissance flight or flights over South Yorkshire. However, it is more likely that the spying, or intelligence gathering, was done by Germans who came to Thorncliffe in the late 1930s and who were advising Newton Chambers on the modernisation of the foundry. The spy must have been there before 1938, when work began on building the tank factory, which is not labelled on the map. Whether or not there were spies involved, the Germans missed the most important target of all, because they never found out about the existence of the tank factory at Thorncliffe.

*Chapter 12*

# GRANDEUR AND DECLINE

Encouraged in part by what they have read in Catherine Bailey's best-selling *Black Diamonds*, many local people blame 'Manny' (Emmanuel) Shinwell, Minister of Fuel and Power from 1945 to 1947 in the post-war Labour governments of 1945–51, for the decline of Wentworth Woodhouse, which has only recently started to be reversed. In fact, several other factors were at work. Though Lord Shinwell (as he became) was not well disposed towards the aristocracy, we should not forget the impact of death duties, the failure of the Fitzwilliam earls to produce direct male heirs, and the changes in society brought about by the two world wars. All these undoubtedly contributed to the decline, which was only too evident by 1979, when the last earl died. However, Shinwell provides an easy target – a politician who can be vilified, secure in the knowledge that few will stand up for him now.

**Days of grandeur**

The importance of the owners of Wentworth Woodhouse can easily be appreciated when we stand in the park of the estate and survey the scene, especially the vast width of the east front of the house (a Grade I listed building), 606 feet in length and with more than 300 rooms, the park itself, which extends to 180 acres (73 hectares) and once had a boundary wall that was 9 miles in circumference, and the monuments to be seen on the horizon. In particular, Hoober Stand is remarkable, commemorating as it does the defeat of the Jacobite Rebellion of 1745, and the making of peace in Europe three years later. The first of these events was a significant milestone in the life of the future 2nd Marquis of Rockingham. He was only 15 at the time, but felt so strongly that he must 'do his bit' that he ran (or rather, rode) away from home and crossed the Pennines to join the Duke of Cumberland's army and fight for King George (see Chapter 3).

As the architecture and the landscape indicate, most of what we see at Wentworth Woodhouse today was built and shaped in the eighteenth century. The 2nd Marquis was Prime Minister in 1766, and again in 1782, and it was in his time that the east front was completed and the magnificent stable block built. He was followed by no less than seven Earls Fitzwilliam, and their wealth and power were still evident in the early twentieth century.

William Charles de Meuron Wentworth-Fitzwilliam, the 7th Earl Fitzwilliam (1872–1943) succeeded to the earldom on the death of his grandfather, the 6th Earl, in 1902, and he was one of the richest men in Britain. He had several estates in England and in what is now the Republic of Ireland. He owned the coal that lay in abundance under the South Yorkshire estates, as well as the mining equipment and the houses and cottages inhabited by hundreds of miners, estate employees and agricultural workers. He maintained a stud to provide racehorses and hunters. He had a priceless art collection and a fifty-room house in Mayfair. He would probably be worth around £3 billion today, and he controlled the lives of those who worked for him (and their families) to an extent that would be unthinkable now.

There are many stories about Wentworth Woodhouse that emphasize its size. In 1937, the 'Court and Society' column of a national newspaper informed its readers that:

> Nervous guests are reputed to have tried the experiment of having a paper trail along passages to guide them back to their rooms; and another tale is that, during Doncaster week, when the host and hostess always entertain a large party, a manservant decided to test the distance covered while performing his duties, and his four days' work registered over fifty miles on a pedometer.[1]

In the 6th Earl's time, there had been eighty-four employees at 'the Big House'. A photograph, taken in 1890, shows a housekeeper and eight maids. Another, taken ten years later, shows sixty outdoor and non-domestic staff. A third, taken in 1902, shows eleven woodyard staff, but there were also gardeners, park keepers, deer keepers, gamekeepers, grooms, poultry men and many others. Wentworth Woodhouse was large enough to accommodate the largest of parties, and there were no less than three royal visits, in 1886, 1891 and 1912.[2]

**Male outdoor staff,** *c.* **1900.** *Pauline & Michael Bentley*

Successive owners of Wentworth Woodhouse were on the reformist rather than the conservative wing of British politics. In the eighteenth and early nineteenth centuries, they were Whigs and then Liberals, but that tradition eventually foundered on the rock of Gladstone's advocacy of Home Rule for Ireland in the 1880s. As a result, the future 7th Earl became a Conservative and was the Tory MP for Wakefield from 1895 to 1902, when he took his seat in the House of Lords. Nevertheless, the Fitzwilliam family continued to enjoy its favourable reputation in England in the nineteenth and early twentieth centuries, despite the advent of democracy and radical changes in society (especially in the relationships between master and servant). Indeed, the family continued to be regarded with respect and affection, even in the southern counties of Ireland, where hatred of the Protestant Ascendancy ran deep. Many country houses belonging to the British aristocracy went up in flames during the Irish War of Independence of 1919–21, but Coollattin House and Carnew Castle still stand, though they no longer belong to the Fitzwilliam family.

The Wentworth-Fitzwilliams were entrepreneurs and industrialists, as well as landowners. If the headquarters of their agricultural enterprises was in Wentworth, the beating heart of their industrial empire was in nearby Elsecar, where there had been collieries since the 1750s and ironworks from the 1790s until the 1880s, and which by the early twentieth century employed many hundreds of miners. The importance of this can be seen even today at the Elsecar Heritage Centre, where what remains of their private railway runs alongside the old workshops and the Newcomen Pump (believed to be the oldest surviving steam engine of its kind in the world in its original location). 'Billy Fitzbilly', as the 7th Earl was known, was also an adventurer and innovator. His taste for adventure was demonstrated in 1904, when he bought a steam yacht and set off to Cocos Island in the Pacific in search of buried treasure,[3] while shortly after his return he founded the Sheffield Simplex car company. In its day the Simplex was a rival of the Rolls-Royce, though the factory where it was built closed in 1925.

### Sad decline

If Wentworth Woodhouse continued to enjoy days of grandeur in the early twentieth century, it experienced a decline after 1943, when the 7th Earl died. He was succeeded by his son Peter, who was killed in an air crash in 1948 along with his lover Kathleen (or 'Kick') Kennedy, the sister of the American President John Kennedy.

Open-cast mining under the direction of Emmanuel Shinwell dealt another hammer blow. As Minister of Fuel and Power from 1945 to 1947 in the post-war Labour government of 1945–51, Shinwell was in charge of the mines, which needed to produce unprecedented quantities of coal in the late 1940s as a result of a balance of payments crisis and the exceptionally cold winter of 1946/47. His plan for solving the problem included extending open-cast mining into the grounds of Wentworth Woodhouse.

During the war, the coal mines had been under state control, and the Labour Party was committed to nationalising the means of production, if elected when peace was restored. Shinwell was a committed socialist. The son of Jewish immigrants, he had grown up in a two-room flat in a tenement block in Glasgow and had little time for rich coal owners like the 8th Earl Fitzwilliam, though the latter had served with distinction during the war and was popular with local people, including his miners. There was an inevitable confrontation between the new Labour minister, who had served the requisition order and was responsible for steering the Coal Nationalisation Act through the House of Commons, and the owner of Wentworth Woodhouse.

Shinwell told Parliament that he wanted to work 371,000 tons of coal at Wentworth, of which 220,000 tons was 'good-quality Barnsley coal', urgently required for the railways; the method to be employed was open-cast mining. Earl Peter Fitzwilliam strongly disagreed. He commissioned an expert report from Sheffield University, which found that, if Shinwell's plan was implemented, the coal obtained would be 'very poor stuff' and 'not worth the getting'. Accordingly, Fitzwilliam proposed an alternative scheme, involving drift mining, but Shinwell thought this would take too long. He pressed ahead with his own proposals, despite the Earl's extensive lobbying and his success in obtaining the support of the local miners.

The open-casting went ahead, first in the fields between the parish church and the kitchen gardens. Then, in April 1946, when the gardens immediately behind the west front of the mansion were threatened, Earl Fitzwilliam travelled to London to see Clement Atlee, the Prime Minister, to seek a reprieve. But the bulldozers had already moved in, working through the night with lamps on the arms of the excavators, moving 130 tons of earth every hour. By morning, the gardens were like a moonscape, while some of the spoil was dumped in large heaps next to the Long Terrace. Countess Maud watched helplessly.

As Catherine Bailey notes, 'open-cast mining in the vicinity of the House continued into the early 1950s; and much of the woodland and the formal gardens were not

E.L.S.165-24. Wentworth Woodhouse From The Gardens

**The gardens in front of the Baroque mansion.** *Pauline & Michael Bentley*

replaced.'[4] As she also says, this was widely resented in South Yorkshire. Some local people will still not hear a good word said about Shinwell, and it is difficult not to agree that there was an element of vindictiveness about his decision. But it also has to be said that, whatever else it does, open-cast mining does not cause subsidence. Further, the Fitzwilliam family was compensated financially for what was done, and much of the land affected was eventually reinstated.

There were other factors that contributed to the decline of Wentworth Woodhouse as a great country estate. One of these was the cost of litigation, for there were at least two serious disputes in the Fitzwilliam family, in 1902 and 1951. On the death of the 6th Earl in 1902, some members of the family contended that William de Meuron Wentworth-Fitzwilliam was not the legitimate son of his father, Lord Milton, who suffered from epileptic fits and died at the early age of 37 in 1877, before he could inherit the Wentworth estate and the earldom. One story is that Lord and Lady Milton had had a baby girl and soon after her birth substituted her with a boy.[5] Another is that Lord Milton had taken his son for a walk (they were then still living in Canada) and then had had an epileptic fit and went home without him. A search party said they had eventually found the infant unharmed on a haystack.[6] But Milton's siblings contested his eligibility, claiming that Milton and his wife Laura had picked up the

**Open-cast coal mining in the gardens of Wentworth Woodhouse in 1947.** *Roy Young/ Wentworth Garden Centre*

wrong baby and that Billy was not his real son. They claimed he was a substitute, or 'changeling', and therefore had no right to succeed as 7th Earl. Eventually, members of the family withdrew their claim.

The 8th Earl had no male heir, and the Wentworth estates and the earldom passed to a distant cousin, Eric, who became the 9th Earl. But as he died without issue in 1952, another major family dispute occurred and resulted in a full hearing in the Royal Courts of Justice, before Mr Justice Pilcher. This time the trial concerned a dispute between Toby and Tom Fitzwilliam, who were brothers, as to who was entitled to succeed to the earldom and the entailed estates[7] on the 9th Earl's death. Tom alleged that Toby, though older, was illegitimate, while Toby claimed that his parents had undergone two ceremonies of marriage, and the earlier had preceded his conception. The first ceremony had been conducted in Scotland, where the common law was (and is) different, but after a full hearing, the judge held that it did not in fact amount to a valid marriage, partly because the parties had not lived in Scotland for the requisite twenty-one days prior to the wedding ceremony. After a dispute resolved by the Probate Divorce and Admiralty Division of the High Court, the title and dependant estates then passed to Tom (who became the 10th Earl), who also died without issue. The legal expenses involved in this case must have been considerable, though it is difficult to think that these alone would have been an intolerable burden for a family that was still so wealthy. It is also unclear as to who precisely paid the costs. The earls ceased to use Wentworth Woodhouse as their principal private residence in 1952, while the earldom itself became extinct on the 10th Earl's death in 1979.

Meanwhile, Wentworth Woodhouse had undergone several changes of use. It had already been used as a training depot and headquarters of the Intelligence Corps during the Second World War (see Chapter 11). Then the Ministry of Health proposed to requisition it as housing for homeless families. To prevent this, the 8th Earl attempted to donate it to the National Trust, who declined to take it. Subsequently, the 7th Earl's sister, Lady Mabel, who was a socialist, arranged for West Riding County Council to lease most of the mansion, leaving forty rooms for the Fitzwilliam family. Thus, from 1949 to 1979, the house was home to Lady Mabel College, which trained female PE teachers. The college then merged with Sheffield City Polytechnic (now Sheffield Hallam University), which eventually gave up the lease in 1986 due to high maintenance costs (and, by some accounts, because many of the students considered Wentworth too remote from the high life of Sheffield). By 1990, the house had fallen into a very poor state of repair, and needed millions spending on it. The division of the family estates on the failure of the main line of descent meant that a way of life had been lost, something that meant a lot to local people in particular. Although the buildings survived, they were no longer the heart of a community and an enterprise, controlled and directed by a family who, in general, commanded respect and loyalty – even affection.

In 1989, the Fitzwilliam trustees decided to sell the house and the area immediately surrounding it, but retain the majority of the estates in South Yorkshire. A buyer was found for the house in the businessman Wensley Haydon-Baillie, but he was eventually overwhelmed by debt, and the house was repossessed by a Swiss bank. In 1999, it was sold for £1.5 million to Clifford Newbold (1926–2015), a former architect from London,

**A lacrosse team from Lady Mabel College.** *Elma Casson*

and his sons. They lived in the west front from 1999 to 2017, started a programme of restoration and began to open the house for guided tours.

### The Newbold family versus the Coal Authority

The Newbolds alleged that subsidence due to mining operations near the house had caused substantial structural damage. On tours of the house, visitors were assured by the guide that Mr Newbold had sued 'the Coal Board' on three occasions, and on each occasion he had won, but that the Coal Board had not yet paid a penny. Many people must have believed this, just as they believed that Mr Newbold was due to receive around £40 million in compensation, because this is what he told *Country Life* in 2010, as well as Dan Cruickshank in 2011 when he interviewed the owner for a BBC film, *The Country House Revealed*. Yet the truth is more complicated.

They lodged a claim for the cost of remedial works, estimated to be in the region of £100 million, in 2012, and this was heard by the Upper Tribunal (Lands Chamber) in April 2016. However, in its decision dated 4 October 2016, the tribunal found that the damage claimed for was <u>not</u> caused by mining subsidence.[8] It is estimated that the cost of the litigation on this occasion was in the region of £3 million.

The first two paragraphs of the judgment contain an excellent summary of the history of Wentworth Woodhouse and the effects of coalmining in the local area upon it, while paragraphs five and six summarise the issues before the tribunal, and the arguments put by each side. The judge referred to the fact that 'the house and its associated structures are now in a state of deterioration which the claimants attribute to subsidence caused by the effects of coal mining'. He explained that 'beneath the house and its landscaped park lie the productive seams of the South Yorkshire coalfield which had been mined in the area at surface outcrops from the early middle ages'. He referred to the fact that the Fitzwilliams' ancestors had owned Wentworth Woodhouse since Norman times, and were mining coal there by 1750; the invention of Newcomen's 'steam powered engine' allowed deeper mine shafts to be sunk in the eighteenth and nineteenth centuries to meet 'the insatiable demand created by the industrial revolution'. By the 1920s, 'deep seams were being exploited under the park and close to or under the buildings and structures at Wentworth Woodhouse', and latterly, 'the 1947 nationalisation of the coal industry brought intensified mining beneath the park and formal gardens which continued until the 1960s'.

All this was agreed; but the issue now was whether any of the deterioration in four selected areas was 'subsidence damage' within the meaning of the relevant Act of Parliament, so that the Coal Authority was responsible – one of these being the south terrace wall and another being the Camellia House. Moreover, the judge identified that 'the real debate [was] not simply whether subsidence damage had occurred at any time, but whether such damage was the result of a renewed phase of ground movement occurring since the 1990s, long after conventional expectations would have ruled out historic mining as a cause of damage'.

The Newbolds had contended that most of the damage was at least likely to have been caused by the collapse of old mine workings as a result of flooding, following the cessation of pumping in the South Yorkshire coalfield in the 1990s. On the other hand, the Coal Authority asserted that ground movement caused by mining had ended long ago and that Wentworth Woodhouse was largely stable, with the damage visible in the four relevant areas 'being either historic or attributable to a variety of other causes, including neglect and decay'.

The outcome turned on expert evidence, and both sides produced structural and mining engineers to support their arguments. In the end, the judge preferred the evidence presented by the Coal Authority, and he concluded that the 'mechanism of damage' relied on by the Newbolds did not explain the damage complained of. In particular, it was more likely that the critical Parkgate seam was already damaged to a substantial extent in the 1940s. The suggestion that further subsidence had occurred in more recent times was implausible, and there was no convincing evidence that changes that had taken place since 1999 (when the Newbolds purchased the property) were a result of mining subsidence. Technically, the judge left it open for the parties to make further submissions; for all practical purposes, the case had come to an end.

By the time judgment was given, Clifford Newbold and his son Paul had already died, and in any event, Clifford had already decided to sell up. The property was put on the market in 2014, and in March 2017 it was sold to the Wentworth Woodhouse Preservation Trust for £7 million. By this time, the cost of repairing the mansion block was estimated to be anything from £40 million (the figure put forward by Clifford Newbold when interviewed by *Country Life* in 2010) to £100 million (the figure claimed at one stage during the litigation with the Coal Authority).

Fortunately for all of us, the buyer was a trust whose purpose is to conserve the great house and 83 acres (34 hectares) of garden for the local community and the nation.

# NOTES AND REFERENCES

## Chapter 1: The 1st Earl of Strafford

1. Radcliffe, Sir George, *The Earl of Strafforde's Dispatches and Letters with an essay towards his Life* (1739).
2. Wedgwood, C.V., *Thomas Wentworth First Earl of Strafford 1593–1641*, Phoenix, London, 2nd edition (1961, first pub 1935).
3. Hunter, J., *South Yorkshire*, Volume 2 (1831), J.B. Nichols & Son, London, p. 95.
4. British Newspaper Archive, *The Sketch*, 27 December (1905), 'Household Goods'.
5. Wedgwood, op. cit.
6. Wedgwood, op. cit, p. 361.
7. Hyde, Edward, Earl of Clarendon, *The History of the Rebellion*, Volume 3 (1702–1704), Oxford University Press, p. 191.
8. Harman, R. & Pevsner, N., *The Buildings of England: Yorkshire West Riding: Sheffield and the South*, Yale University Press, New Haven & London (2017), p. 727.
9. Information supplied by Jonathan Addy.
10. Gatty, R., 'Lord Strafford's Burial-place', *Cornhill Magazine*, July (1905), pp. 104–109.
11. Morley, C., 'Whose Body Was It?', *Yorkshire Journal*, Issue 40 (2003), pp. 90–5.
12. Fox, G. (ed), *The Three Sieges of Pontefract Castle*, Old Hall Press, Leeds (1987).
13. These 'siege' coins were the first to be struck in Charles II's name. On one side they bore the words *Dum Spiro, Spero* ('Where there's life there's hope'); on the other, *Post Mortem Patris pro Filio* ('After the death of the father, [we are] for the son'). After the Restoration, this became Pontefract's motto. See the town's loyal address to Charles II, Fox, op. cit, pp. 155–6.
14. Hunter, op. cit, p. 98.

## Chapter 2: … Across the Sea to Ireland

1. Details of Thomas Watson-Wentworth's visit to his Irish estates will be found in the Irish General Accounts 1707–1713 (WWM 758) and Irish Timber Accounts (WWM 760) in the Wentworth Woodhouse Muniments in Sheffield Archives.
2. Jones, M., 'The Expansion of a Great Landed Estate: The Watson-Wentworth South Yorkshire Estate, 1695–1782', in M. Jones (ed) *Aspects of Rotherham: Discovering Local History*, Volume 3, Wharncliffe Books, Barnsley (1998), pp. 80–98.
3. The two surveys were by Moland in 1728 (WWM A769) and William Hume in about 1730 (WWM A768) in the Wentworth Woodhouse Muniments in Sheffield Archives.
4. See, for example, Jones, M., 'Coppice wood management in the eighteenth century: an example from County Wicklow', *Irish Forestry*, 43 (1986), pp. 15–31 and Jones, M., 'The Absentee Landlord's Landscape: The Watson-Wentworth Estate in Eighteenth-Century Ireland', *Landscapes*, 1:2 (2000), pp. 33–52.
5. WWM A65 in the Wentworth Woodhouse Muniments in Sheffield Archives.

## Chapter 3: The 1st Marquis of Rockingham's Journal, 1723–50

1. Bridges, J., *History and Antiquities of Northamptonshire*, Volume II (1791), Clarendon Press, Oxford, p. 102.
2. F/WW/1-502, in Northamptonshire Record Office.
3. *Victoria County History of Northamptonshire*, Victoria County History, London (1906), p.178.

## Chapter 4: The 2nd Marquis and the American Colonies

1. Cruickshank, Dan, *The Country House Revealed*, BBC Books, London (2011).
2. Owen, John B., *The Eighteenth Century, 1714–1815*, Rowman & Littlefield, Totowar, New Jersey (1974), pp. 228, 283; and Albemarle, George Thomas, Earl of, *Memoirs of the Marquis of Rockingham and his Contemporaries* (1852), Richard Bentley, Elibron Classics edition, Boston (2007).
3. Wilderson, Paul, *Governor Wentworth and the American Revolution*, University Press of New England, Hanover, New Hampshire (1994), pp. 67, 74–7, 83.
4. Bloy, Marjorie, *Rockingham and Yorkshire, the Political, Economic and Social Role of Charles Watson-Wentworth, the Second Marquis of Rockingham*, unpublished PhD thesis, University of Sheffield (1986), pp. 391, 405, 443–4.

## Chapter 5: Keppel and His Column

1. Langford, Paul, *A Polite and Commercial People*, Clarendon Press, Oxford (1989), p. 547.
2. Bloy, Marjorie, *Rockingham and Yorkshire, the Political, Economic and Social Role of Charles Watson-Wentworth, the Second Marquis of Rockingham*, unpublished PhD thesis, University of Sheffield (1986), p. 246.
3. Hoffman, Ross J.S., *The Marquis, A Study of Lord Rockingham, 1730–1782*, Fordham University Press, New York (1973), p. 351.
4. *The Trial of the Honourable Augustus Keppel, Admiral of the Blue Squadron: At a Court Martial Held on Board His Majesty's Ship Britannia*, Ulan Press, Lexington (2012).
5. www.historyofparliamentonline.org.
6. Guttridge, G.H., *English Whiggism and the American Revolution*, University of California Press, Berkeley (1966), p. 55.
7. Butterfield, Herbert, *George III, Lord North and the People, 1779–80*, G. Bell & Sons Ltd., London (1949), p. 48.
8. *Minutes of the Proceedings at a Court Martial, Assembled for the Trial of Vice-Admiral Sir Hugh Palliser*, Bart Gale, Farmington Hills, Michigan (2012).
9. Howse, Geoffrey, *A Brief Guide to the Fitzwilliam (Wentworth) Estates & the Wentworth Monuments*, Trustees of the Fitzwilliam Wentworth Amenity Trust, Estate Office, Wentworth (2012), p. 64.
10. All newspaper references are taken from the British Newspaper Archive.

## Chapter 6: The Park, Gardens and Menagerie at Wentworth Woodhouse

1. John Cole engraving of 1728, Bodleian Library, University of Oxford.
2. WWM A1273, in the Wentworth Woodhouse Muniments collection in Sheffield Archives.

3. Pococke, R., *The Travels through England of Dr Richard Pococke, 1750*, Volume 1, Camden Society, Westminster, edited by James Joel Cartwright (1888).
4. Young, A., *A Six Months' Tour Thro' the North of England, 1768*, W. Strachan, London (1771).
5. Eyres, P. & Lynch, K., *On The Spot: The Yorkshire Red Books of Humphry Repton, Landscape Gardener*, New Arcadian Press, Leeds (2018), pp. 14–15.
6. See, for example, Eyres, P. (ed), 'The Wentworths: Landscapes of Treason and Virtue: the gardens at Wentworth Castle and Wentworth Woodhouse in South Yorkshire', *New Arcadian Journal*, No. 31/32, Summer/Autumn 1991, pp. 77–129.
7. John Cole engraving of 1728.
8. *Illustrated London News*, 8 September 1888, p. 284.
9. Jones, M., *Protecting the Beautiful Frame: a History of the Sheffield, Peak District & South Yorkshire Branch of the Council for the Protection of Rural England*, Hallamshire Press, Sheffield (2001), pp. 103–104.
10. WWM A1273, in the Wentworth Woodhouse Muniments collection in Sheffield Archives.
11. Jones, J. & Jones, M., *Wentworth Gardens: an illustrated History*, Green Tree Publications, Rotherham (2002).
12. The film has been deposited in the Yorkshire Film Archive by Chapeltown and High Green Archive, Film I.D.: YFA 2304.
13. WWM A1273, in the Wentworth Woodhouse Muniments collection in Sheffield Archives.
14. Pococke, op. cit., p. 58.
15. The menagerie records are all in the Household Account Books in the Wentworth Woodhouse Muniments in Sheffield Archives.

**Chapter 7: Wentworth, the Fitzwilliams' Estate Village and Elescar, their 'Model' Industrial Village**

1. Jones, M., 'Combining Estate Records with Census Enumerators' Books to Study Nineteenth-Century Communities: The Case of the Tankersley Ironstone Miners *c.* 1850', *Local Population Studies*, No. 41, Autumn 1988, pp. 13–27.
2. Clayton, A.K., *Hoyland Nether*, Hoyland Nether Urban District Council (1973).
3. Jones, M., 'The Mapping of Unconsidered Trifles: A Yorkshire Example', *The Local Historian*, 14.3 (1980), pp. 156–63.
4. Tremenheere, S., *Report on the Mining Population in parts of Scotland and Yorkshire* (1845), pp. 25–6.
5. Medlicott, I., 'Elsecar: the Making of an Industrial Community', in B. Elliott (ed), *Aspects of Barnsley: Discovering Local History, Volume 5*, Wharncliffe Publishing, Barnsley (1998), pp. 149–72.
6. Jones, M., 'A Sponsored Migration from Staffordshire to Hoyland in the Mid-nineteenth Century', in B. Elliott (ed), *Aspects of Barnsley: Discovering Local History, Volume 5*, Wharncliffe Publishing, Barnsley (1998), pp. 119–36.

**Chapter 8: The Family's Paternalistic Concern for their Employees and Tenants**

1. Mee, G., *Aristocratic Enterprise: The Fitzwilliam Industrial Undertakings 1795–1857*, Blackie, Glasgow (1975), p. 187.
2. Addy, S.O., *A Supplement to the Sheffield Glossary*, The English Dialect Society, London (1891), p. 13.
3. Wentworth Woodhouse Muniments WWM A1419, St Thomas's Day/Collop Monday records, in Sheffield Archives.
4. National Library of Ireland, Fitzwilliam Emigration Books MS4974 and 4975, transcribed by Jim Rees (2006) in 'From Carnew to Canada: tenants in the civil parish of Carnew listed in the Coollattin estate management books 1847–56', *Carnew Historical Society Journal*, pp. 81–105.
5. A detailed examination of the Fitzwilliam emigration scheme will be found in Rees, J., *Surplus People: The Fitzwilliam Clearances 1847–56*, Collins Press, Cork (2000); and a study of County Wicklow before and after the Great Famine will be found in Hannigan, K., 'Wicklow before and after the Famine', in Hannigan, K. & Nolan, W. (eds), *Wicklow: History and Society*, Geography Publications, Dublin (1994). We are also grateful for the personal views of Kevin Lee, local historian, and expert on the Fitzwilliam Wicklow estate.
6. Elliott, B., *South Yorkshire Mining Disasters, Volume 1, the Nineteenth Century*, Wharncliffe Books, Barnsley (2012).
7. *Sheffield Independent*, 1 November 1856.
8. Mee, op. cit., Chapter 8, pp. 139–56.
9. We are grateful to Val Bintcliffe for locating the Barrow Hospital inmates in the 1871 and 1891 censuses.
10. Jones, J. & Jones, M., *Wentworth Woodhouse Gardens; an illustrated history*, Green Tree Publications, Rotherham (2002), pp. 39–41.
11. Wentworth Woodhouse Muniments, WWM/A/38, in Sheffield Archives.
12. Wentworth Woodhouse Muniments, WWM/A/1654/2, in Sheffield Archives.

**Chapter 9: Earl Fitzwilliam, Cocos Island and the Treasure of Lima**

1. The National Archives, BT 110/222/10.
2. Cooke-Yarborough, G.E., *The Cruise of the Véronique R.Y.S. to the Pacific Ocean, 1904–05*, journal and press cuttings, Doncaster Archives, The Cooke-Yarborough Collection DZ/MZ/30/Y1 (1904); and Smith, David, T., 'El Dorado', *Blackwood's Magazine* (1932), pp. 843–50. See also, Cooper, Stephen & Moorhouse, John, *Earl Fitzwilliam's Treasure Island* (2016).
3. Campbell, Sir Malcolm, *My Greatest Adventure*, Butterworths, Oxford (1931), pp. 67–72.
4. Plumpton, Cdr James, *Treasure Cruise, the Voyage of the Vigilant to Cocos Island*, London (1935), p. 93.
5. *The Times*, 31 July 1934.
6. Hancock, Ralph & Weston, Julian A., *The Lost Treasure of Cocos Island*, Thomas Nelson & Sons, New York (1960), pp. 155–6; and *Hartlepool Mail*, 20 August 1934.
7. *The Times*, 9 July 1936; and *The Manchester Guardian*, 25 March 1939.

**Chapter 10: Celebratory Events**
1. Household Accounts (WWM/A/34), in the Wentworth Woodhouse Muniments in Sheffield Archives.
2. WWM A1273, in the Wentworth Woodhouse Muniments in Sheffield Archives.
3. Joseph Woodcock's 'journal' is used with the kind permission of Kathleen Westgate, one of Joseph Woodcock's descendants.
4. *Illustrated London News*, 8 September 1888, pp. 283–90.
5. *Rotherham Advertiser*, 27 June 1891.
6. *Rotherham Advertiser*, 11 February 1911.
7. *Rotherham Advertiser*, 11 February 1911.
8. *Rotherham Advertiser*, 6 July 1912.
9. The 1912 royal visit is described in detail in Bailey, Catherine, *Black Diamonds: the Rise and Fall of an English Dynasty*, Viking, London (2007), chapters 12–14, pp. 110–52.
10. Smith, David, T., 'A Yorkshire Christmas', *Blackwood's Magazine*, December 1934, pp. 73–81.
11. *Rotherham Advertiser*, 29 November 1913
12. Behan, Paddy (n.d.), *Part of This Place: The memoirs of Paddy Behan and his lifetime association with the Coollattin estate and the Village of Shillelagh, Co. Wicklow*, privately published.

**Chapter 11: Some Military Uses of Wentworth Woodhouse**
1. Se'night is an archaic word meaning a week.
2. See Chapter 2.
3. Donnelly, F.K. & Baxter, John L., *Sheffield and the English Revolutionary Tradition, 1791–1820*, in Pollard, S. & Holmes, C. (eds), *Essays in the Economic and Social History of South Yorkshire*, South Yorkshire County Council (1976), pp. 104–107.
4. Young, Roy, *The Big House and the Little Village*, Wentworth Garden Centre, 3rd edition (2011), p. 134.
5. Young, op. cit., p. 134.
6. *Sheffield Evening Telegraph*, Monday, 20 July 1914 (extract from British Newspaper Archive).
7. www.yorkshirefilmarchives.com/film; and www.hitchcocksmotorcyles.com.
8. Van der Bijl, N., *Sharing the Secret: The History of the Intelligence Corps 1940–2010*, Pen & Sword, Barnsley (2013).
9. Van der Bijl, op. cit., pp. 132–3.
10. www.bbc.co/history/ww2peopleswar/stories/.
11. In 2017, the *Musée du Debarquement no. 4 Commando* in Ouistreham (the port of Caen) staged an exhibition, and a film, concerning the French servicemen who trained at Spean Bridge, prior to the D-Day landings in June 1944. Vila was probably one of these. Spean Bridge is about 10 miles from Fort William.
12. Fletcher, Llewellyn C., *Translating the Devil: Captain Llewellyn C. Fletcher Canadian Army Intelligence Corps in Post-War Malaysia and Singapore*, Gordon D. Feir, Lulu Publishing Services, Morrisville, North Carolina (2014).

13. Fletcher, op. cit., p. 80.
14. A Quonset hut was a prefabricated, corrugated metal hut, based on the earlier Nissen hut, but developed in the USA. The writer was probably referring to Nissen huts, but understandably, since he was from Canada, called them by the North American name.
15. Fletcher, op. cit., p. 81.
16. Fletcher, op. cit., p. 82.

## Chapter 12: Grandeur and Decline

1. Doncaster Race Week was when the St Leger was run, *The Observer*, 12 September 1937 (Courtesy of the British Newspaper Archives).
2. Young, Roy, *The Big House & The Little Village*, Wentworth Garden Centre (2011).
3. Cooper, Stephen & Moorhouse, John, *Earl Fitzwilliam's Treasure Island*, CreateSpace (2016).
4. Bailey, Catherine, *Black Diamonds*, Viking, London (2007), Chapter 33.
5. Bailey, Catherine, op. cit., Chapter 3.
6. Bond, Michael Shaw, *Way Out West: On the Trail of an Errant Ancestor*, McCleland & Stewart Ltd., Toronto (2001), pp. 223–36.
7. An entail was a type of settlement, whereby the ownership of land passed down through the generations in accordance with the terms of the settlement rather than in accordance with the laws of inheritance, or, for that matter, the terms of the current occupier's will. In this case, it meant that the land concerned passed down from eldest son to eldest son.
8. The law report is at 2016 UKUT 432 (LC).

# INDEX